THE THREE MUSKETEERS:
D'ARTAGNAN'S TALE

Borgo Press Books by ALEXANDRE DUMAS

Anthony
The Barricade at Clichy; or, The Fall of Napoleon
Bathilda
Caligula
The Corsican Brothers (with Eugène Grangé & Xavier de Montépin)
The Count of Monte Cristo, Part One: The Betrayal of Edmond Dantès
The Count of Monte Cristo, Part Two: The Resurrection of Edmond Dantès
The Count of Monte Cristo, Part Three: The Rise of Monte Cristo
The Count of Monte Cristo, Part Four: The Revenge of Monte Cristo
A Fairy Tale (with Adolphe de Leuven & Léon Lhérie)
The Gold Thieves (with Countess Céleste de Chabrillan)
Kean
The Last of the Three Musketeers; or, The Prisoner of the Bastille (Musketeers #3)
Lorenzino
The Mad Marquis (with Emmanuel Théaulon & Ernest Jaime)
The Mohicans of Paris
Napoléon Bonaparte
Queen Margot
Richard Darlington (with Prosper Dinaux)
Sylvandire
The Three Musketeers (Musketeers #1)
The Three Musketeers—Twenty Years Later (Musketeers #2)
The Tower of Death (with Frédéric Gaillardet)
The Two Dianas (with Paul Meurice)
Urbain Grandier and the Devils of Loudon
The Venetian
The Whites and the Blues
The Widow's Husband; and, Porthos in Search of an Outfit
Young Louix XIV

RELATED DRAMAS:
The Queen's Necklace, by Pierre Decourcelle
The Seed of the Musketeers, by Paul de Kock, A. Guénée (Musketeers #5)
The San Felice, by Maurice Drack
The Son of Porthos the Musketeer, by Émile Blavet (Musketeers #4)
A Summer Night's Dream, Adolphe de Leuven & Joseph-Bernard Rosier
The Three Musketeers: D'Artagnan's Tale, by P. de Kock & A. Guénée
The Widow's Husband; and, Porthos in Search of an Outfit: Two Dumasian Comedies, edited by Frank J. Morlock

THE THREE MUSKETEERS: D'ARTAGNAN'S TALE

BASED ON CHARACTERS CREATED
BY ALEXANDRE DUMAS

PAUL DE KOCK &

ADOLPHE GUÉNÉE

TRANSLATED BY FRANK J. MORLOCK

THE BORGO PRESS
MMXIII

THE THREE MUSKETEERS: D'ARTAGNAN'S TALE

Copyright © 2005, 2013 by Frank J. Morlock

FIRST BORGO PRESS EDITION

Published by Wildside Press LLC
www.wildsidebooks.com

DEDICATION

For my dear friend, John Cordell

CONTENTS

CAST OF CHARACTERS	9
ACT I	11
ACT II	58
ACT III	103
ACT IV	138
ACT V	177
ABOUT THE TRANSLATOR	203

CAST OF CHARACTERS

D'Artagnan

Athos

Porthos

Aramis

Marquis de Franconnard

Count de Grammont

Planchet

An Officer

A Soldier

A Servant

A Fisherman

The Marquise (Angelique)

Helene

Pelotte

The Superior

La Tourière

ACT I

The court of an inn. Large open door. At the back; to the right a pavilion, window facing the audience; to the left, the buildings; you can read—AT THE ETERNAL TURKEY, Chapon, Restaurants—to the right, a bench before the pavilion. To the left, a bench against the house.

PLANCHET (emerging from the pavilion)

Yes, Milord, as soon as travelers come, I will inform you—that's agreed.

(he shuts the door)

A gold coin—that's right, now there's someone who is generous. I don't often have luck like that.

PELOTTE (emerging from the inn)

Planchet! Planchet! Hurry up, will you, they're asking for you in the kitchen, they're asking for you in the hall, they're asking for you in the cellar—

PLANCHET

Might as well say they're asking for me everywhere—but I can't cut myself in three parts—I'm already being worked to death.

PELOTTE

Ah! Lazy bones! I advise you to pity yourself—and in that case, what will I say—all the work of the house will fall on me!

PLANCHET

Oh! But you, Pelotte, you are strong—and besides, it's not the same with women as it is with men.

(sings)

Women, Miss, I do assure you—are proud of their strength, you see. So it is!

Masterpiece of nature, they must endure more than we. Passionate to please, at work.

They go to it tirelessly. And if you imagine they are all sweaty. They're ready to start all over again.

(speaks)

But as for me, who has no share of this beautiful half of creation, I am beginning to have enough of the profession of waiter at an inn at my relative Champon's, who pinches me when I let the roast burn, who whacks me when I miss a sauce, and who roughs me up when I break a plate. Who cares be to be pinched, whacked, and beat up every day? Those are my wages—which they pay me on time—for goodness' sake. Oh, I am paid punctually!

PELOTTE

Ah! Ah! This poor Planchet.

PLANCHET

And besides that, always so many people in the inn. Finally, today—you don't know where your head is.

PELOTTE

So here are the gay blades who need us. There's no more than a fat pullet, and that's reserved for a great lord who is going to arrive later.

PLANCHET

Good enough! The travelers who come after or before will be satisfied.

PELOTTE

Your relative will send you to get provisions.

PLANCHET

Thanks, I know the tip he'll give me when I return from the market—

(he gestures with his feet)

PELOTTE

Why are you so simple? Why, you bought us rabbits instead of hares.

PLANCHET

Miss, that's not my fault. They had no hares.

SOLDIER (entering)

Water—a room—wine, wine—

PLANCHET

Good—more customers—if they're hungry, it's gonna be nice.

PELOTTE

Escort these soldiers—you will offer them omelets—cheese—

SOLDIER

Hurry up, will you, waiter?

PLANCHET

Coming—

COUNT

They say that in this inn nothing is lacking, so they must love us and serve us properly.

(They go into the inn with Planchet.)

PELOTTE

But where in the world are we going to put all this company? It's all sauce. As for me, I'm not like Planchet. The more it is in a bustle, the more I like it.

COUNT (emerging from the Pavilion)

No one yet. I am getting very worried.

PELOTTE

Ah! There's the young Lord—who came this morning. Happily he hasn't asked to eat—

COUNT

Tell me, young women—two ladies haven't come—traveling without escort—incognito?

PELOTTE

Sir, as for incognito—I saw only an egg dealer who passed with his wife and donkey just now.

COUNT

(aside)

Helene promised me she would convince the Marquise to come say goodbye to me—oh!

Whatever the dangers that threaten me, I will not leave France without seeing her one last time.

PELOTTE

After that, we are still expecting more company—there's a great lord who's reserved a room—perhaps he'll bring some ladies—he's the Marquis de Franconnard.

COUNT

The Marquis de Franconnard—he's going to come here?

PELOTTE

Yes, sir—with his attendants and animals—otherwise put: his household.

COUNT (aside)

Ah! If we were to meet her—let's run ahead—let's try to warn them.

(to Pelotte)

Young lady, I'm leaving—if these ladies come, escort them to this pavilion, and advise them not to show themselves—you understand.

(He leaves by the left.)

PELOTTE

Oh! That young lord hasn't thought of eating because he's in love, I wager. And these ladies he's waiting for—why, there are two of 'em—what's he going to do with two of 'em—for him alone? Ah, heck, after all, we have folks who eat two steaks instead of one.

D'ARTAGNAN (enters covered with dust, rapier at his side)

An inn—ah, that's not bad—for I cannot do any more from weariness and hunger. Let's go in.

PELOTTE

More company! Ah, he's a very young man—he's nice.

D'ARTAGNAN

A serving girl. Now that's my line. Hello, girlie.

(he kisses her)

PELOTTE

Well! Sir—for goodness sake—now that's manners—you're pretty enterprising for a kid.

D'ARTAGNAN

A kid—sonofabitch! I'll let that go 'cause you're nice-looking, but it will cost you again.

(He kisses her again.)

PELOTTE

Ah! From the moment that's the tip you get, it will do—what does the gentleman want?

D'ARTAGNAN

A dinner, some rest, a good room, a nice bed, good wine—and you in the bargain if it's possible.

PELOTTE

Ah, indeed—this child is a demon—how do they let you travel alone, so young—? Aren't they afraid you'll get lost?

D'ARTAGNAN

I didn't ask permission—heavens, do you want to know my

story? In four words, this is it: I was born at Artagnan of a noble family, but not very well to do. My good parents have done for me all that they could do—I received an education worthy of my ancestors—I ride a horse, I fight—I get drunk, I gamble—and with all these characteristics, should I remain at my family's expense? Come on, would you?

(sings)

One fine day I said to myself, I have to get out of here. I'm sixteen years old, and bold, courageous, and smart as well. Time's come to leave the nest. I already yearn to be a jolly fellow. That's from my family. More than one escapade was committed by my ancestors. My family was gallant, brave, very amorous, and very old. In my turn, I intend to do all my daddy once did.

PELOTTE

You are totally funny—and where are you going like this?

D'ARTAGNAN

Where am I going? I don't have a clue—probably to Paris—that's where they hold court. I've a shilling in my pocket, a rapier at my side—with that you can go anywhere.

PELOTTE

Ah—you want to go to court—with only one shilling—I think it costs much more—

D'ARTAGNAN

But, in the meantime, I'm hungry—give me a room and a meal, my little—what's your name?

PELOTTE

Pelotte, at your service, sir—

D'ARTAGNAN

Pelotte! Why I really like that name. Go, my plump Pelotte, you heard me—some dinner, quick.

PELOTTE

That's real embarrassing, go! We've got so much company—anyway, I'll go see—I'm going to try to find you a little out-of-the-way corner. Here—sit down on this bench.

(she points to the bench in front of the pavilion)

D'ARTAGNAN

Very well! Oh! I'm not difficult.

(sits on the bench)

I'm going to take a little nap. Let me know when my dinner is ready.

(he stretches out on the bench.)

PELOTTE

Yes—sir—sleep a bit—

(aside)

I don't know where I'm gonna hide him. Suppose I put him in my garret. Oh! No—they'd think nasty, stupid things—they have such capable tongues.

ARAMIS (dressed a bit more plainly, sword at side, enters)

Ah, I'm going to find a shelter at last! Providence was watching over me—it never abandons its elect.

PELOTTE (aside)

Heavens, yet another raw youth.

ARAMIS (bowing grandly)

Miss, I really ask your pardon for the liberty I am taking—but can I find lodging here?

PELOTTE

Shucks, since this is an inn—

ARAMIS

Excuse me—because I am not in the habit of taking trips.

PELOTTE

Oh! I can plainly see that.

(aside)

What a difference from the other one—he seems reserved—you'd say he was a little priest.

(aloud)

Are you coming from a great distance, young man?

ARAMIS

From my uncle's château, four leagues from here—I am the Chevalier d'Herbelay, but you mustn't mention that, because if they knew I was here—

PELOTTE

Oh, right, you are hiding? You've played some farce—you've seduced some young girl—perhaps?

ARAMIS

Oh, Miss—for goodness sakes—what do you take me for?

(sings)

Never yet to a woman have I been seen to cast my eyes. For them I have in my soul

Only a feeling of respect—

I am modest, I am well behaved,

Thank God—the beautiful sex causes me loss of sleep.

When I see a pretty corsage

I do this quickly

(covers his eyes)

So heaven be blessed.

PELOTTE (aside)

He's a little hypocrite—I like him better than the other one—

ARAMIS

My desire has always been to take up the priesthood—I'd like to be an abbe, but my uncle, who was a military man, intends to make me a Musketeer.

PELOTTE

Heavens—why that's nice, that is—

ARAMIS

As that's not to my taste; this morning, I slipped out of the château—without saying anything to anybody—and I'd be striding along still if hunger and weariness weren't forcing me to stop here.

PELOTTE

Ah! You are hungry?

(aside)

Now there they are—all hungry now.

ARAMIS

Would you kindly indicate to me a room where I can rest in peace and say my grace.

PELOTTE

A room—the thing is, you see—we've got a good crowd here and I don't know what to do to put you up—except maybe to put you in the barn where there are already six nurses.

ARAMIS

Ah! For goodness sake! Put me with nurses—expose me to seeing worldly things—I don't want that.

PELOTTE (aside)

Why is he—?

(aloud)

Here, Sir, wait a bit. If you would please to sit on this bench, I'll try to find an out-of-the-way place where they don't have anything which will shock you.

ARAMIS

That suffices, Miss—I will wait—I'm going to rest here—I really ask your pardon for all the trouble I'm giving you—

(He goes to sit at the left.)

PELOTTE

Heavens! That's my job.

(aside)

He's nice too. It's a shame he's so timid. Ah, it's the other one over there that I'll have trouble dealing with, but where in the devil am I going to put all of them?

ATHOS (running to Pelotte)

Ah! Finally—They've lost my trail.

PELOTTE

Yet another schoolboy. Ah, why indeed, it's raining them today—they've played truant.

ATHOS

Who are you calling a school boy! Know, my sweet, that I am the Count de la Fère, and that I won't hear of anyone lacking respect to me.

PELOTTE

Bah! This is a little count—really—and why then are you running away if you are a real count?

ATHOS

First of all, wench, that's none of your business—but I actually intend to tell you because I need you.

PELOTTE

What have you done to fear being punished?

ATHOS

What have I done—? By Jove, I've fled my paternal home.

PELOTTE (aside)

Another one, Ah, indeed, why they've all got the same idea.

(aloud)

Is it because they wanted to make a musketeer of you?

ATHOS

Quite the contrary. Oh! I intend to be a soldier, I do. I want to serve—I want to become an officer—general—Marshall of France— ,And would you believe my parents want to make a priest of me!

PELOTTE

My goodness—just the opposite of the other one.

ATHOS

Me—go into clerical orders! Never—oh—it's glory that I need—

(sings)

Still quite young, I felt in my veins my blood boil, as soon as I heard of our French, of our great captains—near me, telling of great deeds. I fear the wrath of my parents, and fleeing them I tremble at each step.

But I feel in my warrior's passion, that I won't tremble on the battlefield.

PELOTTE

Ah, why this one'll make a hero.

ATHOS

Now, listen. I've got a well-furnished purse—quick, a room and a good meal—after that, I'm leaving for Paris.

PELOTTE

Ah! Yes, a room and a dinner—they all ask for the same thing. But our inn is full, and hold it, there are already two young travelers like you, waiting for a room and a meal.

ATHOS

Let 'em wait, I want to be served first. Since I've got money—Hold on, this is for your trouble.

(gives her money)

PELOTTE (aside)

This must be a real Count! Trapped.

(aloud)

But suppose there is no place?

ATHOS

You'll find one for me. Come on, wench, go prepare my room and order my dinner, get going I will wait here.

PELOTTE (aside)

He's astonishing, but he must be obeyed.

(aloud)

I'm going to see, sir—keep waiting—Rest somewhere. This one's no villain—but the first one is the one I like best—he kissed me twice.

(goes into the inn)

ATHOS

Yes, yes, I'm going to rest—I ran so much—I am pooped out.

(approaches D'Artagnan's bench)

It seems this one was worn out as well—say there, Sir, make a little room for me—he didn't hear me—he sleeps hard—let's look elsewhere.

(goes to Aramis' bench)

Ah—we're sleeping, too. But he doesn't take up the whole bench.

(sits beside Aramis)

And for the moment this will rest me, too.

Ah—they want to make a priest of me—I will have a ball uniform and I will make conquests—oh! Women—glory—

(dozes off)

PORTHOS

(appearing at the door of the inn and stopping to read the sign, "The Eternal Turkey"—)

Chapon, restauranting meals for a hundred customers on foot or on horseback— Now that's my business— Let's enter the Eternal Turkey—they ought to eat well here, and I am hungry!

Ah, here I am free at least, and here I am my own master. Oh! How amusing to no longer do anything except my own will—my parents wanted to oppress me—they were tyrants—they put me on bread and water under the pretext that I fought with everybody. Heck, if I am strong—that really has to be of use to me for something—

I broke the door of my room—I demolished the gate in my garden—and here I am—ah, what, why is there actually no one in the inn? Hola—waiter—anybody.

PLANCHET (coming in weeping)

Here! Here! It's true—what do you wish, sir—?

PORTHOS

I wish—I wish—what's this one weeping about? What did they do you, my lad? Did they beat you? Where is your adversary? I'm going to rough him up—it won't take long to do his business.

PLANCHET

You are really kind, sir—but you see, it's my relative who beat me—Chapon, the master of the inn—on the pretext that I broke two plates again—as if plates were not made to be broken.

PORTHOS

Ah! If he's your relative—look—give me something to eat—plenty to eat—I've got an enormous appetite.

PLANCHET

To eat! It's that we've got almost nothing.

PORTHOS

Oh! I'm not difficult: put a big shank of lamb on the spit and I'll content myself with that.

PLANCHET

A lamb shank for you alone?

(aside))

What a little glutton—what'll he eat when he's fifty?

PORTHOS

Come on—hurry up—I'm going to lie down while waiting.

(pushing him)

Well—get going will you—muttonhead.

PLANCHET (aside)

A shank—if he has a small Neufchatel cheese, he'll be lucky.

(goes into the inn)

PORTHOS

Now let's rest.

(going to the bench on the left)

Ah, the seats are taken—let's go on the other side.

(goes to D'Artagnan's bench)

Still more company—and I don't see more benches. So much the worst—this one here's all by himself—say there, comrade—move over a bit. Give me some room. Ah, you pretend you don't hear me. I'm going to put you in the space between the bed and the wall.

(he takes D'Artagnan by the legs, places them on the ground, and sits beside him.)

ARAMIS (still sleeping)

Huh? What—dinner—ah, yes—go eat.

PORTHOS

Who sleeps, dines, dear friend—and I'm going to do like you while waiting for my shank to be skinned.

(dozes off)

(Angelique and Helene enter from the rear, wrapped in large cloaks and coming forward stealthily.)

TWO WOMEN (singing low)

Here it is, I think

That he'll be found

Be confident.

He must be here.

ANGELIQUE

Ah, my dear Helene—I feel that I was wrong to grant this rendezvous to the Count—how many dangers I'm exposing myself to—and him, too—if he should be recognized.

HELENE

But this poor young man—because he loved you before your marriage—is that a reason to make him despair now?— Why, Cardinal Richelieu, who bears such a tender interest toward you, forced you to marry the Marquis whom you do not love.

ANGELIQUE

Ah, actually, that's the reason he gave him to me for my husband.

HELENE

And because Mr. de Grammont continued to love, to tell you about it, the Cardinal on the slightest evidence pretends he's conspired with Mr. Cinq-Mars—has signed an order to take him to the Bastille.

ANGELIQUE

Poor Count! He is innocent, no doubt of that, but the Cardinal is powerful; and so as not to be locked up in the Bastille, Mr. de Grammont must expatriate himself.

HELENE

Before leaving France, he desires to say a last goodbye to you—where's the harm in that? The Marquis believes you are in your aunt's château, and besides, am I not here, with you—to ward off perils that might strike you?

ANGELIQUE

Dear Helene, how to repay so much friendship?

HELENE

Doesn't my life belong to you, Madame—haven't you brought me up, protected me, me a poor orphan with no fortune, no support?—ah, I am very happy when I am able to prove my devotion to you.

ANGELIQUE

But I don't see the Count, and no one is here to guide us.

HELENE (looking at the two benches)

Ah! Madame—see, there—a nest of schoolboys.

ANGELIQUE

Indeed—they are resting—happy age—at the end of a long stroll they came here.

HELENE

But they are very nice, all four of them.

(sings)

See each of them resting.

And each one smiles in his sleep.

At that age all is rosy

You're happy even when you dream.

In their thoughts—life

Offers neither pain nor turmoil

Love embellishes it

The path is soft and covered with flower.

ANGELIQUE (singing)

Poor children! Let's talk low so as not wake them up.

TOGETHER

Let's talk low.

So as not wake them up.

PLANCHET (emerging from the house)

No more shank—only some fish—and—ah, heavens, two beautiful travelers.

HELENE

My friend—don't you have a young lord here who's waiting for some ladies—and who told you they would ask for Mr. de Mergy?

PLANCHET

Ah! Yes—yes—Madame—a young man—quite generous—here's the pavilion where he was—but made impatient that you hadn't arrived, he left to go find you.

ANGELIQUE

How annoying.

PLANCHET

Yes—come Madame—don't remain in this court where you might be seen.

ANGELIQUE

As soon as that young man arrives, let him come find us.

PLANCHET

Don't worry, ladies—oh! He won't fail.

(Helene and the Marquise enter the pavilion.)

PLANCHET

These are high-flying ladies—I've just received another whack for a cracked bottle—thanks, I've had enough of this house—I'm packing my bags—but before I do that, I'll have to tell this young guy who's so hungry that he won't have his lamb shank—heavens—there are four of them—the other one has had kids.

ARAMIS (dreaming)

Holy Madonna, pray for me.

PLANCHET

They're dreaming aloud.

ATHOS (dreaming)

Battles—glory—a sword—

PLANCHET

This one, too.

PORTHOS (dreaming)

One shank, two shanks, three shanks.

PLANCHET

He's merely asking for a whole sheep.

D'ARTAGNAN

For me—one mistress—two mistresses—three mistresses.

PLANCHET

Right, that one wants as many mistresses as the other wants shanks.

D'ARTAGNAN

Oh! She will be mine, and if anybody thinks of vying for her with me—

(he wakes up)

Who is it permitted himself to sleep in my bed? What, they come into my room without warning me—

PORTHOS

Ah! Sonofabitch—you've woken me up.

D'ARTAGNAN

(rising)

Observe that great horn! Why did you slip into my bed?

PORTHOS

Your bed—it's damned hard.

ARAMIS (to Athos)

Sir, would you be so kind as to get back—you are suffocating me.

ATHOS (rubbing his eyes)

Ah! What a bad customer—I've had enough of it.

(he rises)

D'ARTAGNAN (looking at the other)

Ah! Ah! What comic faces—

ATHOS

What's this gentleman got to laugh about?

ARAMIS

Why's he looking at me like that?

THE OTHERS

Waiter—anybody—dinner—something to eat—we are hungry.

PLANCHET (coming forward)

Here, gentleman, here—ah—it seems you are no longer sleeping—you were sleeping nicely just now—you were sleeping, pistol by your head.

PORTHOS

See here, imbecile, my shank—

D'ARTAGNAN

My dinner, by Jove—or I skin you.

ARAMIS and ATHOS

My dinner—right away.

PLANCHET

Gentleman, don't get worked up—you must grasp that it's not my fault—I'm not the one who ate up all the provisions of this inn.

D'ARTAGNAN

Ate up the provisions? What's that mean?

PORTHOS

I don't like jokes of this sort.

PLANCHET

It means there's nothing more in the inn than a pullet—nothing more—as to the rest, no meat, no fish—nothing.

D'ARTAGNAN

A pullet? Well—I will content myself with that—you'll serve me that—

PORTHOS

I would have preferred a shank—but still—anyway, give me the pullet.

ATHOS

I ask your pardon, gentlemen, but this pullet will be mine.

D'ARTAGNAN and PORTHOS

Huh?

ARAMIS

Gentlemen, I'm desolate to vex you—I never fail anyone—but I will not endure that others fail me.

D'ARTAGNAN

Well—we are going to laugh a bit then.

PORTHOS

I get the pullet, sonofabitch.

OTHERS

Mine—mine.

D'ARTAGNAN

Gentlemen, we have swords—fate will decide it—

OTHERS

Accepted.

PLANCHET (aside)

Come on—here they are about to fight over a fowl which someone else has got.

THE FOUR YOUNG MEN

What a great outfit.

What pleasure to unsheathe

We must earn our dinner at sword's point.

(The music continues; they fight changing adversaries from time to time. Planchet watches them trembling.)

D'ARTAGNAN

Have at you, sir—why, you don't do badly for your age.

ARAMIS

You are very honest—you take that, fellow.

PORTHOS

By Jove—why, you've got the hang of it—

ATHOS

Why—yes—and you—you are tough, you are.

MARQUIS (appears at the back)

Stop! Stop!

D'ARTAGNAN (putting up his sword)

Company! This is unbearable. You cannot amuse yourself even for a moment—

MARQUIS

What's all this mean?—two duels in broad daylight in this inn—and these are punk kids—schoolboys who allow themselves to scrap.

ATHOS

Kids.

ARAMIS

Schoolboys—

PORTHOS

I want to smash him.

D'ARTAGNAN

Sir, by what right do you come to meddle in our affairs?—if we desire to fight—

MARQUIS

By the law which gives me my duty, gentlemen—know that I am a gentleman ordinary of His Majesty, and grand Squire of the Cardinal.

ALL

Of the Cardinal! Oh! The devil!

HELENE (half-opening the window)

I seemed to hear—

D'ARTAGNAN

From the moment Monsieur is a gentleman ordinary—

MARQUIS

And sometimes extraordinary—

HELENE

It's the Marquis—she's lost if he sees her—

(she shuts the window)

MARQUIS

I repeat to you, do grace to your youth, if you weren't brazen—

THE FOUR YOUNG MEN

Huh—

MARQUIS

I mean brats! I would have you arrested—but your age makes me look on this as a prank—screw it, children—because the Cardinal is not joking about dueling—why, look—why were you fighting on all sides?—for I suppose you had a reason—ordinarily one fights for something.

D'ARTAGNAN

I indeed think we had a reason and an excellent one—we were fighting over who would eat—

MARQUIS

A pullet—

PLANCHET

Yes, the one we were keeping for Milord, and these young gentlemen were fighting over who would eat it.

MARQUIS (laughing)

Ah! Ah! Ah! That's very funny—what they were fighting over, the pullet that I'm going to eat—

Oh! Oh! I find that whimsical. Gentlemen, yet once more,

attempt, at least, to fight for a plate that remains to you.

D'ARTAGNAN

We will fight for you, Milord.

MARQUIS

Thanks, gentlemen—valet, escort me—let them prepare my meal—ah! Ah! Ah! They were fighting for my pullet?

(He, along with his squire, goes into the Inn—preceded by Planchet.)

D'ARTAGNAN

By Jove! What! It's this villainous gentleman who's going to eat the pullet—and we were fighting for nothing?

PORTHOS

That's eating the fists of rage.

ARAMIS

Would you like to resume your parts, Gentlemen?

ATHOS

He's nice—this little man—he is becoming—

D'ARTAGNAN

We will again—no. Hold on, I don't know if you are like me, but this battle made me see you were all brave—it makes me want to find friends in you.

ATHOS and ARAMIS

Me, too—

PORTHOS

As for me, it's different—it gave me the same desire.

D'ARTAGNAN

We esteem each other—that's something already—now—we need to get to know each other. My name's D'Artagnan, a Gascon gentleman—I'm leaving my paternal home to make my way all by myself, and I'm going to Paris—your turn.

ARAMIS

They wanted to make me a soldier—I wanted to remain free—I escaped, and I'm going to Paris—your turn.

PORTHOS

As for me, it's a different matter—they put me on bread and water—I broke everything, smashed everyone, roughed everybody up—and I'm going to Paris.

D'ARTAGNAN

Oh! This is charming—each of is experiencing the same desire. Yes—freedom to us is dear—and to taste it at leisure we need to start a career that gives glory and pleasures.

(repeat)

Let's swear here and now—if fate brings us together again

To always live as good friends, together.

None of us shall sulk or tremble.

We must be united, it seems to me.

And henceforth, share and share alike

Love, glory, and friendship.

TOGETHER

Yes, henceforth we'll share and share alike!

(repeat)

D'ARTAGNAN

That's over, we're friends—let's hug like knights of old.

(they hug each other)

And now, let's begin to understand each other. Aren't you of the opinion that we must carry off the pullet from this ugly Milord?

THE OTHERS

Oh! Yes. Oh! Yes.

PORTHOS

And if he eats it, he shall not digest it.

D'ARTAGNAN

Then, quickly, to work—one to the kitchen, the other to the

cellar—a third to the office, and the fourth—

PORTHOS

To the spit.

TOGETHER

Let's know how to laugh, drink, and fight.

Let's begin our merry exploits.

We four must play the devil

Since one makes love two by two.

PORTHOS

To the spit.

(Together they go into the house running. At this moment the Count appears at the back.)

COUNT

No one yet—they told me they saw two ladies enter—let's learn if they are there.

(He goes toward the pavilion; the window opens and the ladies appear.)

HELENE (at the window)

Madame—there he is—it's him.

COUNT

I am seeing you again at last—

ANGELIQUE

Ah! Wretch! Save yourself—leave this house this instant, this town—the greatest dangers threaten us—my husband is here—in this inn.

COUNT

What have to fear from him? The Marquis has never thought of being jealous of me—on the contrary, he expresses great friendship for me.

ANGELIQUE

Yes., but the Cardinal has told him that you loved me—anyway, he knows that you ought to be arrested, and if he finds us together that will justify the attitude of His Eminence. Hasten to flee—on our side, we will attempt to avoid attention.

COUNT

To leave without taking away the least pledge of your love!

ANGELIQUE

Here—take this ring—it's a present from the Cardinal—his arms are engraved on this stone—it gives entrance and passage anywhere—it can be useful to you in your flight.

COUNT

You brought it! Oh! Thanks! It will never leave me.

HELENE

And now leave quickly—

COUNT

Goodbye, goodbye.

(He leaves by the back—music.)

HELENE

He's gone. We must think of ourselves now.

ANGELIQUE

If you would open this door with caution.

HELENE

To leave that way—impossible. Everything can be seen from the house and I notice some squire of your husband lingering—this pavilion has another exit to the countryside.

ANGELIQUE

But the door is locked—there's no key.

HELENE

We absolutely must have that key—someone's coming—take care—

(She holds the window half open.)

D'ARTAGNAN (enters—hiding something under his cloak)

I did it.

ARAMIS

I've got it.

ATHOS

Stripped from the enemy!

PORTHOS

There it is—

PLANCHET (hands in his pocket)

And me, too—I have something—gentlemen—take me with you—I will be your squire or your valet—whatever you like.

D'ARTAGNAN

That'll suit; I accept you— You will follow us.

HELENE

These are the young folks of this morning—at that age they might be useful, generous.

PLANCHET

For goodness sake, gentlemen—I engage you not to stay in this inn, for there's soon going to be an uproar here.

D'ARTAGNAN

He's right—let's leave.

HELENE (at the window)

Gentlemen, a word—mercy—

ALL FOUR

A woman!

(they approach the window)

HELENE

Two ladies—who are forced to hide themselves—would like to flee this pavilion by a gate which gives on the country, but they don't have the key—if you could procure it for them.

D'ARTAGNAN

Yes, we can do it! To serve the ladies—okay—we can do it, even if it can't be done.

PORTHOS

But if this lord finds us here—

D'ARTAGNAN

It's a question of serving these ladies—we will think of ourselves once they are saved.

HELENE

Oh! The brave child!

D'ARTAGNAN (to Porthos)

Go ask for the key.

PORTHOS (to Athos)

Go ask for the key.

ATHOS (to Aramis)

Go ask for the key.

ARAMIS (To Planchet)

Go ask for the key.

PLANCHET

Pelotte's the one who's got it. I'm going to go find her.

(He goes into the inn.)

PORTHOS

Here's that gentleman, gentlemen.

HELENE (low to D'Artagnan)

If he comes into this pavilion and finds us, we are lost.

D'ARTAGNAN

Fear nothing, he won't get in there so long as you are there.

(The young folks group before the pavilion.)

MARQUIS de FRANCONNARD (emerging from the house with a dreamy air, letter in hand)

This message that I've just received informs me that Count Grammont has dared to show himself in this town—they even think he's hidden himself in this inn—that's very imprudent, for finally the order to arrest him is published everywhere—myself, if I meet him, I will be obligated to execute it—the Cardinal demands it—I will be angry to do it. That poor young Count, I really like him a lot, and I am convinced he's never thought of my wife.

(he turns)

Ah! There you are, Gentlemen—well! You aren't fighting anymore?

D'ARTAGNAN

No, Milord—we respect your orders too much—

PORTHOS

And besides, it wouldn't be worth the trouble anymore.

D'ARTAGNAN

And that key that never gets here—

MARQUIS de FRANCONNARD

Ah! What is this pavilion—I hadn't noticed it before.

ATHOS

It's a place of lodging.

ARAMIS

Very nice—

MARQUIS de FRANCONNARD

Ah! It's you alone?

PORTHOS

The four of us, if you'll excuse it.

MARQUIS de FRANCONNARD

You four! Excuse me, I would really be comfortable to visit this lodging place—

D'ARTAGNAN (placing himself in front of him)

Ah! Milord—for goodness sake—this lodging is not worthy of receiving you.

PORTHOS

The room isn't made up—

MARQUIS de FRANCONNARD

That matters little. I tell you I wish to visit this pavilion—I'm seeking for a guilty person—I know quite well that it's not you, but he could be hidden unbeknownst to you—

PLANCHET (low to Aramis, slipping him a key)

The key.

ARAMIS (giving the key to Athos)

The key.

ATHOS (to Porthos)

The key.

PORTHOS (to D'Artagnan)

The key.

D'ARTAGNAN

Oh! Joy!

(passing the key to Helene)

Take it—leave quickly.

HELENE

Oh! Thanks—

(She disappears.)

D'ARTAGNAN

If, Milord, a gentleman in ordinary to the king absolutely insists on visiting this pavilion, we have no intention of preventing him—if we only had the time to straighten things up a bit.

PLANCHET

I could go scrub the place—

MARQUIS de FRANCONNARD

No, indeed, yet once more, what are all these details to me? I tell you that I'm going to look around in there, that's all.

D'ARTAGNAN (opening the door)

Oh! In that case, allow me to serve as your guide, Milord.

(he opens the door, looks inside and says, low)

They're gone.

(to Marquis)

Whenever you wish to enter, Milord.

MARQUIS de FRANCONNARD

Why, it's an hour that I've wanted to.

(he enters into the pavilion)

D'ARTAGNAN

Go—look around now—but it's also necessary that you shall be unable to run after us.

(gives a turn of the key)

Make your investigation, sir—

And now, on your way—the rest of you—but proudly, arm in arm.

MARQUIS de FRANCONNARD (at the window)

I was mistaken—there's no one.

(he wants to leave)

Heavens, I'm locked in—

D'ARTAGNAN (who has the pullet on the end of his sword)

You are there actually—stay there! We are going to eat the pullet.

ARAMIS

(pointing to a cheese round at the end of his sword)

With the dessert.

ATHOS (pointing to Bread)

We lack nothing—useful and agreeable.

PORTHOS (pointing to a skewered cat)

Here's even another sort of game—prepared without doubt for Milord.

PLANCHET (pulling some bottles from his pocket)

And here's the liquid.

MARQUIS de FRANCONNARD

What do I see! My dinner—that's what they're carrying off—help me—folks—stop those young scamps.

D'ARTAGNAN

Bon appétit, Milord.

TOGETHER

Fresh air's agreeable

To dine in freely

We are going to sit down to eat

And drink to your health.

(They file before the Marquis, brandishing their swords, skewering food; Pelotte comes to the door of the inn and looks at them laughing—tableau).

CURTAIN

ACT II

In Paris—a room with very little furniture. Some chairs, a table, a large armoire to the right, a door to the left—one at the back. A window.

At Rise, D'Artagnan is in the act of brushing his hat—Athos examines his cloak, Aramis reads, Porthos cleans his shoulder belt.

TOGETHER (singing)

Let's spruce up

Let's make it elegant

So as to turn heads

Of the young wenches

That we will see

ATHOS (examining his cloak)

The Devil—I notice a clear spot—ah, there's yet another—good—yet one day more of borrowed light.

D'ARTAGNAN

It seems to me your cloak is not badly lit; as for me, the more I rub my felt hat, the less it shines, and this cursed white feather which lowers its head blushing—Aramis, could you loan me yours?

ARAMIS

What would you do with it? It's bald.

PORTHOS

Do like me—replace it with a rabbit's tail that I stole from the cordon of the midwife's bell downstairs.

D'ARTAGNAN

And if the midwife surprised you stealing her rabbit's tail?

PORTHOS

I'd have told her it was the craving of a pregnant woman.

ATHOS

Right—here's my doublet which is damaged now.

PORTHOS

If you've still got your doublet, then you are very lucky—I am widowed of mine.

(he rises and appears in bathing trunks)

ALL

Ah! Ah! He's in a bath outfit.

D'ARTAGNAN

After all, who made this garb indispensable?

PORTHOS

My word, yesterday I was fasting, I would have swapped it for a roast of veal.

ATHOS

Decidedly, we are all in the same boat.

D'ARTAGNAN

On the verge of being her dupe.

PORTHOS

We still had money when we got to Paris.

ARAMIS

Meaning that Athos possessed 200 shillings.

PORTHOS

Since we put everything in common, it comes to the same thing.

D'ARTAGNAN

That money didn't last long—it's Aramis who's the cause of

it—he finishes a prayer book every day.

ARAMIS

Rather it's the fault of this glutton, Porthos, who eats thirty cutlets per week in eight pâtés.

PORTHOS

And this dandy of an Athos who puts to pillage a perfume shop.

ATHOS

Without counting D'Artagnan, who's purchasing an arsenal of rapiers or pistols.

D'ARTAGNAN

Gentlemen, that can at least be of use to us when we shall be musketeers.

ATHOS

Yes! Count on that—our musketeer's sword has not yet been furnished.

ARAMIS

Will you renounce that career?—oh! So much the better, my brothers, persevere in this intention—if you know how sweet life can be in retreat.

ATHOS

No, damn it all, we are not renouncing a thing—but we are despairing of becoming—how to solicit in this worn-out costume?

PORTHOS (pointing to his bathing pants)

This uniform is not received at court.

ATHOS

Decidedly, fortune is not favorable.

ARAMIS

We have sinned—we are punished.

D'ARTAGNAN

What's that mean, by Jove! Regrets, complaints—weakness—so you are not men—

(sings)

Where then are your alarms coming from?

Why are you discouraged?

Do you throw away your weapons when danger arrives?

If fate is fatal to us.

If it refuses us gold

If the present is modest

The future at least remains to us.

We are still rich—

ALL

We are still rich.

ATHOS

Your confidence inflames me.

PORTHOS

It drives away my sorrows.

ARAMIS

Hope is reborn in my soul.

D'ARTAGNAN

Friends, your hopes will never be deceived, for we have for treasures a soul the better hardened. Our valor, our swords—we are still rich.

ALL

We are still rich.

PORTHOS

I feel enthused—this devil of a D'Artagnan always puts us back into a fine mood.

D'ARTAGNAN

Ah! That's cause enough for me—I've got good courage—and I have something.

D'ARTAGNAN

You've got something—what have you got?

PORTHOS

If it could be a crown piece?

D'ARTAGNAN

Ah—you are not there.

ARAMIS

He's sighing—it's love—with whom are you in love?

D'ARTAGNAN

Oh! Gentlemen don't question me. Discretion—that's the main virtue in a lover—

(aside)

And besides, as of yet, I've nothing to tell them—I haven't gotten very far—! Besides—if I spoke to them of the neighbor, they'd pay attention to her—and I prefer to ogle her all alone.

PORTHOS

Ah, Indeed! I'm starving—is there no lunch today?

D'ARTAGNAN

Let's call Planchet.

ALL

Planchet.

PLANCHET (emerging stage left, in a wool bonnet)

The milord's have done me the honor of calling me their servant.

ATHOS

No question—come forward, rascal.

PLANCHET

Rascal—that's not my name, I'm called Planchet.

PORTHOS

You are really dallying, lout—

PLANCHET

Nice—now my name's "lout"?

ARAMIS

Next time be more prompt, my friend—

PLANCHET

Sir, it's not my fault, I was in the act of sewing on a button, for I am threadbare. Oh! Why I am threadbare so that I don't know where it's going to stop?—my breeches are becoming thin—the porter told me they saw it—the day shows through it.

D'ARTAGNAN

The fact is, you lack elegance—you are not worthy of being in our service.

PLANCHET

You think so—it's true, I was better off at the home of my relative Chapon—I had Pelotte to sew on my buttons in those days—but if you would give me the three pounds a month that you promised me—

D'ARTAGNAN

That's fine—we'll see about that later—once we are musketeers—

PLANCHET

I haven't the time to wait!

ATHOS

What's that you say, Clown?

PLANCHET

Clown! Planchet—my name's Planchet—Monsieur de la Fère.

ATHOS

And as for me, my name is no longer La Fère; don't you recall then that to put our parents off the track we've changed our names—that I took that of Athos.

ARAMIS

I, that of Aramis.

PORTHOS

I, that of Porthos—because I carry all that I want to.

PLANCHET

Heavens, I've a craving to call myself Planchines—

D'ARTAGNAN

Only I kept the name of my village—D'Artagnan— Gentlemen, something tells me that our names will be illustrious one day—that they will never perish.

PORTHOS

It's my stomach that is dispirited. Planchet, go find lunch.

PLANCHET

Gladly, gentlemen—if you'll give me some money—

D'ARTAGNAN

What's he saying? What is it you permit yourself to say?

PLANCHET

Heck, I permit myself to ask you for money to have food—

ATHOS

Money—what's the good of that?

ARAMIS

Money is the source of all vices.

PLANCHET

It's also the source of all lunches—especially as the cabaret keeper no longer is giving credit.

D'ARTAGNAN

That's different—in that case—hands in pockets, gentlemen, let's make a collection. Hold out your hat, Planchet.

PLANCHET (holding out his hat)

Here, gentlemen, make a pregnant collection—it will be counted all at once—I'm not going to look.

ATHOS (after rummaging in his pocket)

Here!

(he puts something in the cap without anyone seeing what it is)

ARAMIS

My turn.

(he fumbles in his pockets)

That's all that I possess.

(he put it in the same way)

PORTHOS (rummaging)

Could I by chance have lost—oh! Yes—I have something.

(he puts it in Planchet's cap)

D'ARTAGNAN

As for me, I don't know if I have—any—here's what I've got.

(placing it in the cap.)

PLANCHET

Ah! We're going to see what this makes.

(shakes his cap)

That's singular, it doesn't ring at all.

D'ARTAGNAN

Count, will you, imbecile?

PLANCHET (fumbling in the cap)

What's this I feel?

(pulling out)

Some—biribiri—a ball of twine—a queen of hearts, and a button—the one I lost.

(the young men laugh)

And you want me to go purchase lunch with that, gentlemen?

D'ARTAGNAN

Come on! Not so much manners—tell the cabaret man that he's to give us the most delicate thing he's got—goose with truffles, wine from Anjou.

ARAMIS

The signs of a nun.

PORTHOS

Fresh pork, and let the dish be served hot, or we will make him perish under a cane.

PLANCHET

Why, it's I who am going to be caned.

D'ARTAGNAN

You heard us. Gentlemen, let's go finish dressing—Porthos, I will loan you a set of breeches.

(sings)

Go find our meal

Make sure it's tasty

We want to sit down to eat

So hurry your step.

PLANCHET (sings)

(aside)

If they hope to feast

Let them draw a thousand sprees

I feel on my return

My basket will be as empty as their pockets.

TOGETHER

Go find our meal, etc.

(The young men go into the room at left.)

PLANCHET (alone)

Go get provisions with this—first of all, the button is mine. Ask for a fowl against a queen of hearts, a basket of wine for a ball of twine, a basket of wine for a ball of twine—O ball—that name reminds me that at my relatives' place there was one whose garret was above my straw mattress: she couldn't turn or utter the least sigh without my hearing her.

(The door opens gently—Helene appears.)

HELENE

I think they've gone out. Ah! There's still someone here.

(She quickly shuts the door and vanishes.)

PLANCHET

But let's put aside these mythological memories—come on—come what may—I'll risk it—if the wretched cook is inflexible, I still have three sous. I will buy them a Saveloy.

(He leaves.)

HELENE (alone, emerging from the armoire with a large basket in hand)

He's gone. Poor young people—! I heard everything, learned everything. Their difficulties, their distress—chance caused me to discover in my apartment a door which was blocked only on my side and only hidden by this armoire—

Knowing that I had for neighbors those young folks, who in an inn had saved my protectress, I felt the desire to pay the debt we had contracted to them.

Poor Angelique—forced to remain so close to her spouse—for several days I haven't had any news of her—something bad might have happened to her—

Come, drive off these sad thoughts, and let's only think of helping my young neighbors in the future—they are gentlemen of good families—I know their names now.

Let's quickly arrange the table.

(she pulls a table forward)

A nice white table cloth—

Now the provisions.

(she runs to the closet and return with provisions)

Oh, they'll be happy to find their lunch ready—there indeed is what's needed. I would like to enjoy their surprise. They are going to shout miracle, magic—still what could be more natural!

(sings)

They saved Angelique that I adore.

I owe them as much care today

And it's an extreme joy for my heart

To come here.

To succor them.

(noise coming from the left)

There they are—be mysterious,

Let's keep this secret.

Let them still be unaware—for the wealth that is silent

Gives a double payoff

It's doubly a good deed.

(She vanishes through the armoire at the moment the four young men arrive.)

D'ARTAGNAN

The others.

(entering having finished dressing)

Here we are now as elegant as can be in our house coats—and when Planchet gets here—

PORTHOS (noticing the table)

Eh! Why he's been back—look, gentlemen. What a sight!

ATHOS

A furnished table.

ARAMIS

All we ordered.

D'ARTAGNAN

Plague! Planchet has actually done things very nicely. Would never have thought with what we gave him he would be able to purchase all that.

ATHOS

The cabaret keeper allowed himself to be softened up.

PORTHOS

Let's go—to table—and long live good cheer!

ALL

To table!

TOGETHER

Come on.

Drink up.

Let this party

Be complete

And without respite

Let's have a toast to Holy Credit!

D'ARTAGNAN

I don't know if it's because this lunch only cost me a Queen of Hearts, but I find it delicious.

PORTHOS

And the wine excellent.

ARAMIS

It's manna in the desert, my friends.

PORTHOS

Leave us in peace with your manna—it's actually pheasant and golden.

ATHOS

Do you know, gentlemen, that Planchet is not a lad as naive as we thought.

D'ARTAGNAN

I'm so pleased with him that I propose to double his wages—

PORTHOS

I think that we can do that. That won't bother us more—drink up. Drink up.

ARAMIS

Why, we are going to get drunk.

D'ARTAGNAN

Come on, will you, by Jove.

(sings)

What's that you are saying? Men like us will ruin their minds. For two flasks! No down it all, everyone drink up. Let nothing stop us.

PORTHOS (singing)

Yes, from children, let's pillage forever.

From too timid characters.

And bravely act henceforth

Like future musketeers.

D'ARTAGNAN (singing)

We will make others, I believe

When we are king's men.

TOGETHER (singing)

We'll make others, my word

When we are king's men.

D'ARTAGNAN (singing)

Blushing—we'll no longer blush

Before women's eyes.

If, from love, we experience the fires

We will burst in flame

If disdaining our modest success

They play the rebel

Quick to the assault, friends, we'll carry them off.

And if need be—die for them

We will make others, I believe, when we are king's men—

ALL

We will make others, I believe, etc.

(They drink. Planchet enters by the back.)

PLANCHET (without seeing them)

No credit. I was sure of it. Here's the cavaliers—which will represent three services.

(he sees them)

Well—now what do I see? They are gobbling away. They are gorging themselves.

D'ARTAGNAN

Ah! Gentlemen—here's the brave Planchet!

ATHOS

Come forward will you, Planchet, come receive our compliments.

PLANCHET (aside, uneasily)

Compliments?

ARAMIS

You understand marvelously how to order a meal.

PORTHOS

This here is succulent! I will make you my maître d'—when I

have a hotel.

D'ARTAGNAN

The fact is, this repast is worthy of a Cardinal—say then, Planchet—the cabaret keeper is actually a good kid—

PLANCHET

Good kid! Ah! Yes, he received me well, go—when I asked him for credit— Yie! The swine—if ever I go back there—the devil take me if I know where this meal came from.

D'ARTAGNAN (aside)

What's he saying!

ARAMIS

Pretend all you want—very nice—modesty is the attribute of great souls—but to reward you, learn that we have decided to double your appointments.

PLANCHET

Ah! You've doubled my—oh! My God! That's not worth it.— I'd prefer to be reduced and receive something.

ATHOS

Come on, gentlemen—to finish up let's drink to Planchet's health.

ALL

To the health of Planchet!

(They drink then leave the table.)

PORTHOS

Now, to end the day messily, I propose to go fight the town—to go fight the passersby—to go fight the watch.

ATHOS

To try to make conquests.

ARAMIS

In this outfit, that's difficult.

PORTHOS

One is always beautiful after dining well—

D'ARTAGNAN

Yes, but these stitches have a bone to pick with my stockings—who will patch them up for me?

PORTHOS

By Jove, we had actually since yesterday, a stocking mender who set up her cart under our windows. Planchet give her a sign to come up.

PLANCHET

You want me to call a stocking mender?

ARAMIS

Eh! Yes! Hurry up, will you?

(Planchet stands before the window.)

ATHOS

Gentlemen, a consideration—with what will we pay the stocking mender?

PORTHOS (fumbling in his pockets)

With what—

ATHOS

Don't make a pretense of searching, you know quite well you won't find anything.

D'ARTAGNAN

By Jove, Gentlemen, she's a woman—we'll kiss her and she'll give us credit for the rest.

PLANCHET

Here's the stocking mender.

PELOTTE (entering)

Here's the place they were calling me—they need a mender—here I am with my needle, gentlemen.

PLANCHET

I recognize that trumpeting voice and fluty nose.

PELOTTE (looking at Planchet)

Ah! This one has a stupid appearance that I've seen before.

PLANCHET

It's Pelotte!

PELOTTE

It's Planchet!

D'ARTAGNAN

Eh! By Jove! I recognize this little one, too—she's the service girl from the Eternal Turkey.

PELOTTE

Ah—it's my kisser—and the other young men, too—how you meet folks.

(she gives them her hand)

It pleases me to see you again, gentlemen.

PLANCHET

But you, Pelotte, have you come to Paris in that cart below?

PELOTTE

No, it's my shop. Mr. Chapon, our boss, having kicked me out the door of his inn.

PLANCHET

I wager you had cracked something.

PELOTTE

Oh, no—it's not for that, actually.

D'ARTAGNAN

There was some other reason then?

PELOTTE

Because he found—one night—a big saber under my bed.

ARAMIS

A saber—where's the harm in that?

PELOTTE

It's that the saber was in its sheath.

PORTHOS

That's normal.

PELOTTE

The scabbard was hanging from a belt.

ATHOS

That happens all the time as well.

PELOTTE

And the belt hung from a gunsmith.

D'ARTAGNAN

Ah—get out!

PLANCHET

What, Pelotte—you stuffed a gunsmith under your bed?

PELOTTE

It was so he could put back on his clothes. In short, the boss gave me the sack—I fixed up mine, and as I was told pretty girls make their way in Paris, I took the coach. I arrived in this big city, where needle in hand, I am becoming a stocking mender.

(sings)

Really, I don't know

A profession more appealing

All my fun down here

Is to repair the down under

By my skill, I shine

And my diligent needle

Is successful every day

With numerous calves (of legs).

I see near my cart

Many a fop prowling

And even great lords

Who come to offer me their hearts

When they describe their martyrdom

I hurry to tell them

Your hearts are very flattering, gentlemen,

But I prefer your calves.

ARAMIS

She's actually comical, this chubby girl.

ATHOS

Oh, Miss Priest—would you actually not look at a woman—

PORTHOS

As for me, I find her pretty as can be.

PELOTTE

You are really nice, my lords—

D'ARTAGNAN

Lord—Oh! My poor Pelotte, your lords are not dazzling at the moment. We don't have a penny.

PELOTTE

That doesn't matter—I will patch you up gratis—as much as you like.

ATHOS

Truly! You are a nice girl—in that case, I'm going to profit by the opportunity.

PORTHOS

As for me, all the same I have the weight which causes things to become unstitched.

ARAMIS

As for me, skinniness—

D'ARTAGNAN

Planchet—go on all fours.

PLANCHET

On all fours?

D'ARTAGNAN

Obey! As for us, gentlemen—sit on Planchet.

(Planchet reluctantly goes on all fours. The others each place a leg on Planchet.)

D'ARTAGNAN

That's it—present arms—

PLANCHET

Heavens—now there's Pelotte who's going to pass a review of calves.

PELOTTE (threading her needle)

I'm right here—dress your ranks.

D'ARTAGNAN

Say then, you won't sew all four legs together?

PELOTTE (mending one after another)

Have no fear of that!

(sings)

Attention! Today

Thanks to my help

Each leg will be nice

And my needle

By working up your stockings

Will make your step confident.

PORTHOS

Ah—what a wound.

PELOTTE

There's nothing. You, sir, hold still.

D'ARTAGNAN

Ah! First thing—take in the lining.

PELOTTE

You are handsomely fixed.

(spoken)

There that's done.

ALL

Today we can

Thanks to her help

Show a nice leg.

(singing)

And her needle

By mending the holes in our breeches

Has given assurance to our step.

D'ARTAGNAN

We'll pay you for all, one day, Pelotte.

PLANCHET

Yes, when they pay me my wages—that they've doubled.

(sings)

I'm almost upset about it because it will be harder for them to do it.

ATHOS (hugging Pelotte)

Here's something on account.

ARAMIS

This is the only sort of money I have.

(kisses her)

PORTHOS

Here's my largest coin.

(hugs her)

PELOTTE

Ah! Gentlemen, you are very generous.

(aside, approaching D'Artagnan and offering her check)

Well—and as for him, he won't give me a thing.

D'ARTAGNAN

Ah! Hold on, my little Pelotte—you would be sweet to fix up this pair of gloves—take them—you'll show them to me when they are done.

PELOTTE (taking the cuffs)

Yes, sir, gladly.

(aside)

He'll pay me for everything 'en gros'.

ATHOS

Aren't you going out with us, D'Artagnan?

D'ARTAGNAN

No, Gentlemen—I've got a letter to write. I will rejoin you.

ARAMIS

At your ease, I will be at Notre Dame.

ATHOS

As for me, I'm going to get mail.

PORTHOS

As for me, I'll be at the Café Pineapple.

PLANCHET

Pelotte, I will escort you to your cart—I will visit your inside.

TOGETHER

Hearts full of hope

We are leaving with agitated foot

Come run to town

And till this evening

Au revoir.

(All leave except D'Artagnan)

D'ARTAGNAN (alone)

Go beat the pavement, my friends, go seek adventures. As for me, I am staying right here, in the hope that my young neighbor lady will poke her head out the window—I noticed her twice already—and only for a minute—but she looked charming to me—I even thought I recognized her features—where could I have seen her before?

Oh—if she was here—that woman—If we could have a private chat with her— It seems to me I'd be sick with pleasure.

O love—it's so delightful.

(sings)

At any age—it's so sweet

To be in love.

HELENE (outside)

To be in love.

D'ARTAGNAN

To know by one's tongue how to charm.

HELENE

How to charm.

D'ARTAGNAN (listening, then resuming)

A new fire agitates itself in me.

HELENE

For me.

D'ARTAGNAN

And my heart is beating faster—why?

HELENE

Why?

D'ARTAGNAN (spoken)

Oh—why, that's singular—there's an echo in this room—and that echo's got a really pretty voice—let's start over.

(sings)

Ah—my heart just heard—

Also—

HELENE

Also—

D'ARTAGNAN (sings)

A voice sweet and tender. Here.

HELENE

Here.

D'ARTAGNAN

Appear, you that I implore already.

HELENE

Already.

D'ARTAGNAN

Yes, she that I adore is here.

HELENE (appearing)

Is here—

D'ARTAGNAN

What do I see? Is that a dream—? An illusion?

HELENE

No, Mr. D'Artagnan, it's indeed a reality, it's your neighbor—and she's also one of those characters, who, two months ago, received a signal service from you and your friends.

D'ARTAGNAN

Ah! I recognize you now, Madame, you were in that pavilion with another lady.

HELENE

Yes, my benefactress, who at this moment, might still actually be in need of sincere friends—for a letter I've just received from her informs me of new dangers that threaten her—

D'ARTAGNAN

Well, speak, Madame, am I not here, myself and my friends—for whom I answer?

HELENE

Is that actually true, Mr. D'Artagnan? You would consent to devote yourself to the interests of my friend, to brave perils for her?

D'ARTAGNAN

To brave perils—oh! Why that's indeed the nicest thing— Ah— for goodness sakes, I place only one condition on my devotion.

HELENE

And what's that?

D'ARTAGNAN

It's that you tell me your name.

HELENE

Helene.

D'ARTAGNAN

Helene! Oh! I adore that name—to continue, it's that you will allow me to love you?

HELENE (lowering her eyes)

Can one ever forbid such things?

D'ARTAGNAN

Oh! How good you are—and you will love me too—a little bit?

HELENE

Ah! You are going too fast—now—talk seriously—are you courageous?

D'ARTAGNAN

I want to be a musketeer!

HELENE

You are not lacking in cleverness.

D'ARTAGNAN

I'm a Gascon.

HELENE

In that case, listen—it's a question of my protectress—before her marriage, she tenderly loved a young man who's been obliged to flee because he is accused of conspiracy—this young man is the Count de Grammont— Unfortunately, being a girl, my friend attracted the attention of the Prime Minister—furious for not having been heard. It was he who married her to an old and ridiculous lord.

D'ARTAGNAN

That wasn't the way to make her forget the Count—

HELENE

On the occasion of this marriage, the Cardinal made Angelique a gift of a magnificent ring—

She gave it to the Count when he left, but Cardinal Richelieu noticed she no longer was wearing his present; he has witnessed his discontentment— Judge the fix my protectress is in. Happily, the war gave her a little respite—His Eminence left to press the siege of La Rochelle, but he announced he won't be absent for more than ten days—and—on his return—

D'ARTAGNAN

It is urgent that your friend have the precious jewel; if not, she's lost! Well! For that it's necessary to run on the tracks of the Count and demand the ring from him—

HELENE

That's the very thing—we know that the Count has not been able to leave France—he lies hidden in the environs of La Rochelle—he's taken the name of de Mergy—but perhaps—you will have great difficulty in discovering him.

D'ARTAGNAN

We will succeed. I will make it my business.

HELENE

Then, also, give him this letter in which I inform him that he can intrust the ring to you—that he must hasten to yield it to you.

D'ARTAGNAN

This very morning we will leave—we'll kill the horses—we'll be at the frontier in three days—we will find Mr. de Mergy—he'll give me the ring and within the week, I'll be back—

(sings)

To accomplish this task—

Nothing, here, must cost too much

And although this departure pains me,

It is a reward that I want to deserve

Yes, when I go to risk my life

Permit me—it's there, my only desire

A soft look, a hope

Or indeed, alas, a memory.

HELENE

Yes, but for this trip, what's needed above all, is money—and you don't have any—

D'ARTAGNAN (embarrassed)

You think so!

HELENE

I'm sure of it—accept, then, this purse on my friend's behalf—oh—to refuse it would make it impossible for you to serve us—I would no longer believe in your devotion.

D'ARTAGNAN (taking the purse)

Oh—give it to me, give it to me in that case, I will do all that you wish—

HELENE (aside)

He's charming.

(uproar outside)

Someone's coming—it's your friends—I am leaving you—be discreet—prudent—

D'ARTAGNAN (kissing her hand)

And love for life—

Helene—oh—pretty name!

(She goes into the armoire)

(Enter Athos, Porthos, Aramis, and Planchet. Athos has a hollow in his hat. Porthos has only half his cloak—Aramis' arm is in a scarf.)

TOGETHER

To receive this insult, what would they of say of us? What horrible adventure. And what frightful bad luck.

D'ARTAGNAN

And what's wrong with you, by Jove? You are in a fine condition.

ATHOS

Entering the mall, I wanted to fling down a lansquenet, who sent me his bowl in my legs—he refused to cross swords with me under the pretext I was too young—so I fell on him with my fists—we boxed.

ARAMIS

As for me, I unsheathed with a miscreant, who permitted himself to laugh in church. I ran him through his left arm and I received this scratch.

PORTHOS

As for me, I left half of my cloak in the muzzle of a dog belonging to a cook, a shopkeeper who took it ill that I was smelling his merchandise.

PLANCHET

Say then, gentlemen, I will do well to recall Pelotte to fix you up.

D'ARTAGNAN

No question—for you are in no state to travel.

THE OTHERS

Travel?

D'ARTAGNAN

Yes, gentlemen, we are leaving instantly for the frontier—we are going to La Rochelle.

PORTHOS

To do what?

D'ARTAGNAN

I will explain to you, en route—let it suffice you to know that it's in the service of a great lady—who sent me this for our travel expenses.

(he shows the purse)

ALL

Gold.

PLANCHET

They can pay me my wages—

D'ARTAGNAN

We don't have a moment to lose—at the first second-hand clothes dealer we will buy clothes—Planchet will go search for some horses—then—on our way.

CHORUS

Come, let's set out

Time presses, let's not delay

And fortune, I wager

Will follow our steps wherever we go.

PELOTTE

My God! What I just heard—you are leaving.

D'ARTAGNAN

Yes—we are leaving you.

PLANCHET

Goodbye, Pelotte, without waiting longer— We're itching to get outta here.

PELOTTE

Paris begins to displease me. Take me with you. I will follow your steps. I will be your housekeeper. I'll take care of your clothes, your breeches.

D'ARTAGNAN

We give in to your prayers. Come with us, immediately. And we will designate you, my dear, breach mender of the regiment.

TOGETHER

Come, let's get going.

Time presses, don't delay

And fortune I wager

Will follow our steps wherever we go.

(All prepare to leave. Planchet takes the boxes.)

CURTAIN

ACT III

The interior of a poor cottage. To the left, a large chimney—then a door—the door at the back remains open and allows the sea to be seen—to the right, an oven, a table, a bread bin.

COUNT (emerging, dressed in a large hat, he goes to the fisherman who enters from the back.)

Well—brave man—are you bringing me good news? Can I still get a ship?

FISHERMAN

Ah! Heck, Sir, it's very difficult at this moment, I am only two leagues from La Rochelle, which is still in the power of the Protestants.

They are fighting down there and the Cardinal has given strict orders, so that no one can leave the coasts of France.

COUNT

But I am neither an enemy nor a Huguenot, I am a poor proscribed, quite innocent of the accusations against me—

FISHERMAN

Still, my brother has promised me to loan us his boat—in an hour it will be down there in a small hollow hidden by reeds—and I will take you to the closest island.

COUNT

Ah—very good! In an hour, you say?

Yes, sir, oh! Not before—besides, when it gets here, I'll advise you by planting on the shore one of my nets on a stick.

COUNT

Thanks, my friend.

FISHERMAN

I'm going back to my fishing—excuse me for leaving you alone, Sir—

COUNT

Oh! Don't trouble yourself, brave man. I will wait, at your place, for the moment of my embarking.

FISHERMAN

And trust me, don't show yourself outside, for soldiers are devilishly prowling about around here—one could meet them at any moment—

COUNT

I will be prudent.

FISHERMAN

Till we meet again—in an hour—you'll see the stick and the net.

COUNT

Agreed.

(The fisherman leaves the hut.)

COUNT

I am lucky to have found asylum in the dwelling of this fisherman—up to now, I haven't met obstacles in my flight—to those who would have assisted me and asked me who I was, it sufficed me to display this ring, telling them "With the Cardinal!" What would be His Eminence's fury if he knew the present he gave the Angelique was being used to protect me.

Cursed Cardinal—who doesn't want me to love Angelique. While it was all the same to this excellent Marquis. Ah! In my exile, my sole consolation is to think of her and to look at this jewel she wore.

(looks at ring, then strides up and down.)

But who's that traveler? That figure—no mistake—it's the Marquis—the Marquis in this country—! What's he coming to do here? Perhaps he is burdened by orders concerning me—

(Turning back to look)

His steps are heading toward this house—here he is!

MARQUIS (outside, mopping his face)

I am extremely hot and I am very weary—where can I rest?

COUNT (aside)

Let's hide—and try to learn what brings him to these parts!

(he goes into the room at the left)

MARQUIS (at the door)

Ah—this cabin—would you indeed allow me to rest here, brave fisherman.

(enters)

Heavens, why there are no fishermen at all—they are at sea, no doubt—and they have left their door open—it is certain that there isn't much to steal here—my word, I'm going to begin by sitting down.

(he sits)

I thought I was doing a fine thing by sending my servants on ahead—I said to myself, by strolling, I'm going to cut across the road through the grass—I always loved the grass—right up to the grass soup. But I think I wandered away, I must be lost—so much the worse—I will take a guide donkey.

PLANCHET (entering from the rear, carrying four valises and night sacks)

(at the door)

Decidedly I am doing a mule's job— First of all, I'm going to do like our horses did, who collapsed down there. Oh—he—eh! A house—is there hay here?—four pecks of oats, if you please.

MARQUIS

Who's this? I think this wiseguy is asking me for oats? He thinks he's in a stable.

PLANCHET

Can't you answer down there? I am asking you for fodder.

MARQUIS (turning)

Know, wiseguy, that if I had hay, I would keep it for myself. You don't know you are dealing with a lord of the court of France?

PLANCHET (placing his valises on the ground)

Ah—why, wait a sec! Now I remember you, Milord.

MARQUIS

He calls me, Milord—he's recognized me.

PLANCHET

You come to lodge at the inn of my relative, near Chahore, at the Eternal Turkey—

MARQUIS

At the Eternal Turkey. That's me.

PLANCHET (aloud)

And Milord is traveling now in this country?

MARQUIS

My word, my lad, if I am here, it is indeed against my will—I am going to honor you by telling you this although you are only a servant—but when traveling one chats with the first person to come along—that's the way it's done.

PLANCHET

Milord is very frank.

MARQUIS

And besides, I really enjoy talking about my affairs. I tell everybody about 'em—I allow you to come closer.

PLANCHET

Ah! Milord.

MARQUIS

Come on, will you—since I permit it.

PLANCHET (going very close)

Milord!

MARQUIS

Not that close, clodhopper—there, that's fine. You have to know that I have a spouse, a very pretty woman—of whom I am the intrinsic possessor—the Prime Minister, who has the kindness of watching particularly over my honor, didn't he imagine that a young lord was paying court to my wife, he was taken with her extremely and she responded to his passion—

(sings)

The Cardinal dared to tell me

That everyone was laughing at me

Because in secret my spouse was sighing

For this young Lord

Even more, in his extremity of error

He pretended that I was actually—

But the word is not mentionable

But it rhymes with 'household.'

PLANCHET

Oh! I know it is—it's a word in use in all languages!

MARQUIS

In short, the Count, accused of conspiracy, escaped—but the Prime Minister has learned that he's in hiding in this country. So he's given me the order to come here and have this poor Grammont arrested—I would indeed have passed up this favor—if the Huguenots are coming to attack us, we'd have to fight them—and I cannot stand the odor of gun powder—it makes me cough.

PLANCHET

Ah! You were sent to direct patrols searching for this young man?

MARQUIS

As soon as I make myself recognized, but I've arrived, and no one yet, in this country, suspects he has the honor of possessing a person of my importance.

PLANCHET (aside)

I'm going to recount all this to these gentlemen—

MARQUIS (moving away)

I feel better—could you serve me as a guide, you blockhead?

PLANCHET

I, Milord—? I don't know this country any more than you—besides, I am with my masters.

MARQUIS (going to the back)

Ah! You have masters?

PLANCHET

I really think so, I have four of them—so indeed, if one sends me away, I fall back on the three others. But they will never send me away. They are too nice for that.

MARQUIS (aside, looking into the countryside)

Eh! Why, what do I see down there? In the shade of a gooseberry bush? A young girl who's putting on her stockings. Eh! Eh! She has a well-made leg—if she could be my guide. It's a shame that I'm obliged to go give my orders—goodbye, my lad, goodbye.

PLANCHET

Your servant, Milord.

MARQUIS (aside)

What a calf! What a ravishing calf. That little girl pleases me.

(he leaves)

PLANCHET (alone)

(going back)

Old grasshopper, go—how he trots—heavens, you'd say he's going to find Pelotte—who's stopped to fix a stitch.

COUNT (emerging from the room without seeing Planchet)

I know enough, the Marquis has come to execute the Cardinal's orders. I'm no longer safe here and I must leave.— More people—I thought they both had left.

PLANCHET

Oh! Why, he scampers like a mouse.

(noticing the Count)

Ah! Somebody—pardon, Sir, for the liberty I've taken— Eh! Why I'm not abusing myself—those features.

COUNT (aside)

The way he's looking at me—

PLANCHET

Yes, I recognize you, sir—you, too, you came to my relative's place—you were expecting some ladies—you gave me a big tip. You are Mr. de Mergy.

COUNT

What's he saying?

PLANCHET

What luck! The very one we are searching so zealously for— ah—we've got you at last.

COUNT

What's this signify?

PLANCHET

It signifies—oh, you are soon going to know. Don't budge from here. Sir, don't even budge. I'm going to find my masters—we're going to be back. Ah! We've got him!

(he leaves, running)

COUNT (alone)

They've got me, he says—his masters are also directed to arrest me! So, all I find everywhere are enemies—I've got to flee, find another boat.

(preparing to leave)

So long then, France—and perhaps forever!

D'ARTAGNAN (appearing at the entrance door with his friends. They bar the Count's way)

No one can pass!

COUNT

Leave me alone, gentlemen, or if not—

D'ARTAGNAN

I repeat to you that no one can pass.

COUNT

What, Gentlemen, you dare to attempt my liberty! Ah—if I had a weapon.

D'ARTAGNAN

Oh! You misunderstand, Sir, we are not enemies, quite the contrary, it's to do you a service that we are pursuing you—and, thank God—you made us run.

ATHOS

And croak our horses.

ARAMIS

And curse the innkeepers—

PORTHOS

And dine ill.

COUNT

What do you mean?

D'ARTAGNAN

First of all, take this letter—it will accredit us to you.

COUNT (taking the letter)

Helene's signature—the faithful friend of Angelique.

(peruses the letter)

Is it possible—you are sent by her—you've already saved her from a great peril—? Oh! My young friends, pardon my unjust suspicions.

D'ARTAGNAN

Oh—Count, we are very happy to be able to prove to you that we are already worth something—but would you finish reading that letter—it must tell you to deliver a jewel to us.

COUNT (reading)

Indeed—this ring—she would be lost if she doesn't have it to return to the Prime Minister. This ring has protected my flight—perhaps it might be able to save me still, but if it's a question of the well-being of she that I love. I must not hesitate—here's the ring.

(he kisses the ring)

D'ARTAGNAN

Is he lucky to kiss something that comes from his mistress.

ATHOS

As for me, I would also really like to kiss something.

ARAMIS

And we have nothing.

PORTHOS

Not even a sugar barley.

D'ARTAGNAN

We are going to return to Paris—but before leaving, we'd like to know you're safe and report the good news at the same time—

COUNT

The master of this cabana must procure a boat for me—before long it will be near the shore—but will I be able to get there? Wait—down there—see those soldiers scouring the countryside—ah—it's me they're looking for—I've no doubt of that.

D'ARTAGNAN

It's true—impossible to pass so long as those soldiers are there.

COUNT

And the Marquis also has just arrived from Paris, he's charged with the strictest orders—

PLANCHET

I've seen him, Gentlemen—that Marquis—he was here just now—he's the gentleman with the pullet—

ALL

He might be.

PLANCHET

He went to look around, Pelotte—but wait—here's our breaches mender running over this way—she's going to give us news.

PELOTTE (running in breathless)

Ah! By God, it's annoying. Just because I've got pretty eyes—must everyone want to caress us, pursue us, molest us! Ah! Oh—yuck!

That's the way it is, but when it comes to that the gallant will pay me. And bam-bam—when someone attacks—and boom—bam—my person. Ah! I swear it, I won't be so nice. And bam-bam—they'll remember it.

D'ARTAGNAN

What's the matter with you, Pelotte? What rage!

PELOTTE

By God! I've had it with a villainous old goat noble—who absolutely intended to kiss me—but he was so bold—it's astonishing how an old geezer can get inflamed.

PLANCHET

Hell! Naturally, old wood burns faster than green.

D'ARTAGNAN

Where is this gentlemen now?

PELOTTE

Down there—he's looking for me. I got away—he lost me in a thicket.

PORTHOS

Suppose we were to go rough him up.

ATHOS

Propose a sword bout with him.

D'ARTAGNAN

No indeed—no indeed—on the contrary, this fantasy of the Marquis must serve us to save the Count.

COUNT

What are you hoping for?

D'ARTAGNAN

I have my plan—we must draw the soldiers here—that's necessary so you can join your ship without meeting them. Planchet, return to the horses, see they are saddled and bridled. You, Count, go into this little room.

(he opens the door to the left)

A window gives on the countryside; when the soldiers can no longer prevent your flight, I will inform you— You, Pelotte, to the door of this hut—the Marquis will rush to come to rejoin you here.

PELOTTE

Well! If he comes to join me here, he's going to pay court to me.

D'ARTAGNAN

That's as it must be.

PELOTTE

He's going to say stupid things to me.

D'ARTAGNAN

That's as it must be.

PELOTTE

He's going to want to—

D'ARTAGNAN

That's as it must be—what have you to fear? We will be here and I answer for everything.

PELOTTE

Ah! If you answer for everything.

D'ARTAGNAN

As for us, Gentlemen, it's a question of hiding ourselves—I'm going to crouch in the bread bin.

ARAMIS

As for me in this oven—

PORTHOS

And me—in the chimney—

COUNT

Especially, my friends, don't expose yourselves for me—

D'ARTAGNAN

To expose ourselves. Eh! Why that's our joy, it's our glory that's beginning—each to his post and pay attention to orders.

TOGETHER

Don't waste time

Profit, by the moment

Let's hide ourselves around here,

We will all surprise him

She will show herself

And soon as he sees her—

Here, he'll come fast indeed.

(The Count goes inside. Planchet leaves with the valises—the four young men hide.)

PELOTTE

Ah! I agreed to attract this old seducer—if it were not to obey these gentlemen, not often would I wink at this old cuckold.

(she goes to the door)

I see him down there. He's still after me—he's not looking this way—is he dumb! Still, I cannot call him.

D'ARTAGNAN (sticking his head out of the bread warmer)

Sing, and he will hear you.

PELOTTE

Heavens, that's an idea.

PORTHOS (sticking his head out)

Ah! There's no ham in the chimney.

ARAMIS (showing his head)

You can choke in this oven.

ATHOS

My knees hurt.

D'ARTAGNAN

Will you hide very quickly!

(they all disappear)

PELOTTE

I'm going to sing him the breech mender song.

(sings)

One fine day a man was sighing

For a breech mender.

So very much, he ogled her—

That she was ashamed.

She, seeing him on his feet

She saw him before his pants

That put in confusion

The beautiful pants mender—

He's heard, he is coming.

D'ARTAGNAN

Continue.

PELOTTE (sings)

The young man told her straight

As he put his arm around her—

Be my wife, in this day

For me—what a godsend!

Crowns I do not have

But you sew breeches

So in our household no one will say.

There's neither money nor stitches.

(spoken)

He saw me. He's hurrying—

(she goes into the hut)

So of our household no one will say

There's neither money nor stitches.

MARQUIS (appearing in the door)

It's she—it's really she.

(he sings)

Tra la la—la la la la!

PELOTTE

Heavens, he's singing.

(she turns)

Ah—it's you, sir—

MARQUIS (entering)

Yes, delightful traveler, I heard you. And like the sign, you attract the fishes.

PELOTTE

Bah! Are you a fish?

MARQUIS

It's a way of expressing myself—mythologically—you were singing a very witty song.

PELOTTE

It's the song of a pants mender—that becomes me, I'm a pants mender—I am—that's my situation.

MARQUIS

Ah! You are—that's actually an agreeable profession—if I was not a Marquis, I would be a pants mender—for women—you'll see such pretty legs.

PELOTTE

Not always—some are like flutes.

MARQUIS

Hum! Still that's not yours—oh, there's nothing you can do—I've seen 'em!

PELOTTE

Will you shut up?

MARQUIS

What do you want? I adore beautiful legs—they're my passion—I ask myself why nature gave only two legs.

PELOTTE

How many then would you like to have?

MARQUIS

I would never have too many of them to adore. And what are you doing in this country, ravishing breech mender?

PELOTTE (going toward the oven)

What am I doing? What am I doing?

D'ARTAGNAN (low)

I am seeking a fortune.

PELOTTE

Hell—I am seeking fortune.

MARQUIS

You are seeking a fortune? Don't go far from here—you've found it.

PELOTTE

I've found it? Where's it at?

MARQUIS

Look at me.

PELOTTE

What for?—I don't get it.

MARQUIS

Keep looking at me. Know then I am one of the richest Lords of the Court of France—and that if you want to reply to my flame, I will fill your life with gold and silk. I will pet you—

D'ARTAGNAN

Old lecher—

MARQUIS

Huh? I thought someone was calling me—

PELOTTE

Ah—you are telling me this—you want to cajole me—but if I were weak enough to believe you—you would abandon me very quickly.

MARQUIS (aside)

She's softening. Come on, warming, warmly.

(aloud)

No—breech maker of Cynthia and Paphos. You would have been worthy of mending the breeches of Cupid—if he'd worn any—as for me, deceive you—! Fie! First of all, for a pledge of my passion receive this pin!

(aside removing a pin from his shirt)

It comes to me from my great-uncle—who is dead. Fie! He'll never be around to ask for it back.

(aloud)

Take it—

PELOTTE

But, sir—

D'ARTAGNAN (low)

Accept—

PELOTTE

What! You wish to—?

MARQUIS

Allow me to attach it to you—

(he puts the pin on her and kisses her hands)

PELOTTE

Why sir—

D'ARTAGNAN (low)

Let yourself do it.

MARQUIS

It's not all—it's really not enough.

(sings)

Yes, believe me, good-lookin',

I intend to make you happy

You look so cute

Your eyes are so sweet

They increase my ardor.

Once again take this purse

My dollars are in it.

It serves as a start.

But it's not enough.

D'ARTAGNAN (aside)

Take it anyway. He has to pay for his lusts.

PELOTTE (aside)

I'll take it anyway—he has to pay for his lusts.

MARQUIS

For always. Yes, you will be my "love".

PELOTTE

What sir? So many things for me? That makes me all confused.

MARQUIS

You'll get lots more—in return, as for me, I am only asking you now for a tender kiss.

PELOTTE

A kiss! For goodness sake—

D'ARTAGNAN (low)

Let yourself do it.

PELOTTE (aside)

Ah! But—ah, indeed—it's that if I always let myself do it—

MARQUIS (sings)

You cannot know, my darling,

How to refuse my desires

When you are made to please

You must get used to it.

PELOTTE (sings)

Oh, why, yes—a kiss

You seem very tender to me

That, alas, makes me shy.

MARQUIS (sings)

Well! Let me take it

And don't give it.

(they kiss)

D'ARTAGNAN (low)

That's the way it always is. He will pay us for his lusts.

PELOTTE

What a speech. It cannot last forever.

MARQUIS

Forever. Yes, you will always be my love.

(spoken)

Oh! I'm in the fifth heaven—but that's not high enough.

PELOTTE

What do you mean you're not high enough?

MARQUIS

It's at your knees that I want to take my oath to put you in a fine house.

PELOTTE

At my knees? Well! Let's see—put yourself there.

MARQUIS

Here I am, divine—er, what's your name?

PELOTTE

Pelotte.

MARQUIS

Decidedly I am wound up.

THE FOUR YOUNG MEN (all showing their heads at the same time)

Ah! Ah! We've caught you at it, sir.

MARQUIS (on his knees)

Oh, my God—there are people here—in the chimney, under the table—in the oven—in the breadbox—into what a scrape have I stuffed myself.

D'ARTAGNAN (going to the Marquis)

This is very nice, Milord. You are providing us with fine examples.

ARAMIS

To seduce a young girl—

ATHOS

A man of your age.

PORTHOS

With such hair—

MARQUIS (aside, rising)

I'd like to be in a field of nettles.

D'ARTAGNAN (low to Pelotte)

Go join the soldiers—send them here.

PELOTTE

Right away.

(she leaves)

MARQUIS

Still, gentlemen, I don't know by what right—by what right—ah, indeed! Why hold on—it was you who cheated me of my dinner in an inn.

THE YOUNG MEN

Ourselves—Milord.

MARQUIS

So then, it's the devil who sent you here?

D'ARTAGNAN

Ah! Milord, what we've done is a prank of our age—but you, to try to seduce a young innocent! To give her a pin and a purse!

MARQUIS (aside)

Screw it! I am really compromised—and if they go spreading it about—?

D'ARTAGNAN

Frankly, it's really bad—a man of your rank—of your nobility—for we recognize you, too.

MARQUIS

You know who I am?

(aside)

I am going to be shamed, jeered—

D'ARTAGNAN

Certainly, we know quite well we have the honor of speaking to the Count de Grammont.

(The soldiers appear at the back.)

THREE OTHER YOUNG MEN

Greetings to the Count de Grammont.

MARQUIS (aside)

They take me for the poor count—oh! Bravo—I much prefer that—let's leave them in their error.

(The soldiers listen.)

MARQUIS

Well, my word, my friends. Since you know me, I won't seek to deny I am the Count de Grammont.

AN OFFICER (stepping forward)

Then, Count de Grammont, in the name of the King and Milord, the Cardinal, you are my prisoner!

ALL

Prisoner!

MARQUIS

Ah! You are arresting me, Gentlemen?

(aside)

After all, what's this to me? When I get before the Commandant of the town, I'll simply show my orders to get myself known.

D'ARTAGNAN (low to his friends)

The trick is turned—let's go quickly to make the Count de Grammont escape.

(aloud to Marquis)

Count, we are desolated at what has happened to you—we pray you to receive our greetings and regrets.

MARQUIS

That's good. That's good—go, Gentlemen, I will not keep you.

ALL

Greetings to Monsieur de Grammont.

D'ARTAGNAN (low to others)

Now for the other one.

(The young men leave.)

OFFICER

Count, you are going to follow us.

MARQUIS

And where are you going to take me?

OFFICER

To Paris, to the Bastille.

MARQUIS (aside)

The others are gone, I no longer need to feign.

(aloud)

Gentlemen, the time has come to undeceive you. I am not the Count de Grammont.

OFFICER

You are not? You yourself agreed you were just now.

MARQUIS

Just now, I had reasons for that—I am the Marquis de Franconnard sent by the Cardinal—and I can prove it to you.

(shots)

Well—what's that—who's fighting?

A SOLDIER (running in)

Lieutenant, a man protected by four young men and riding a fine horse has just cast himself into a ship. He is, they say, the Count de Grammont.

MARQUIS

Ah! Clumsy that I am! Eh! Certainly that's the Count, since I am not—I have been duped by those four good-for-nothings.

They were conspiring to further the flight of the Count. You must rush after them, arrest them.

SOLDIER

That's what we did, Milord—but we were only able to stop one alone—the others have escaped.

MARQUIS

And where's the one you caught?

SOLDIER

Here he is, Milord.

(they lead in D'Artagnan)

CHORUS

He took his flight

But we ran faster

We'll see if he plans

To escape us again.

D'ARTAGNAN (aside)

Misfortune—it's I who am caught, and I've got the ring.

MARQUIS

Ah—this one will pay for the others. Let's be off, gentlemen.

REFRAIN

He took his flight, etc.

(They lead D'Artagnan, the Marquis strides at their head.)

CURTAIN

ACT IV

The court of a Convent. A large wall at back. To the left, the edifice of the convent; to the right, the garden; near the audience—a thicket, a stone table.

NUN

It's happening—it's happening—My God! One doesn't even have time to say an Ave.

(She vanishes to the right.)

SUPERIOR (emerging from the convent)

Again, some traveler who's coming to us—no doubt—this convent is situated in a deserted countryside—one league around you'll meet no dwelling place—they are often lucky to find shelter here.

NUN (coming back)

Madame—the purveyors to the convent are bringing supplies of dried vegetables.

SUPERIOR

That's fine. And this pilgrim who completed his final day, has he left our holy house?

NUN

At dawn. He wanted to leave yesterday, at night, but I explained to him it was impossible.

SUPERIOR

The rule of this house wills it, and whoever it may be it must not be violated! All pilgrims who seek asylum here must spend eight days in prayer for the rest of our souls

NUN

Eight days—actually that's not much.

SUPERIOR

Especially in this age of perdition, where one sees impious youth preferring worldly pleasures to monastic meditations.

NUN

Like this little pensioner that His Eminence sent us.

SUPERIOR

Yes, Miss Helene, who, since her arrival hasn't stopped shivering.

(looking to the left)

Heavens, there she is heading towards us—even more sad than usual.

HELENE (to herself)

No news from the Marquise—nothing—the whole world is abandoning me.

SUPERIOR

Well, daughter, are you beginning to become reasonable—to please yourself with us?

HELENE

Please myself here? Oh! No, Madame, I'm much bored with it, on the contrary.

NUN (aside)

What impiety!

HELENE

Why are you detaining me here? Why was I taken away from all those I loved?

SUPERIOR

It's the Cardinal's order.

HELENE

Still, you cannot keep me prisoner forever—?

SUPERIOR

The Cardinal will decide.

HELENE

At least let me write to someone who is very dear to me?

SUPERIOR

The Cardinal forbids it.

HELENE

Always that response!

(sings)

Instead of dissipating my ill

When you prolong my sadness

Why do you vex me ceaselessly

With the Cardinal's prohibition?

Vainly you invoke the desire

Of that strict will

On Earth the Cardinal

Cannot forbid what God allows—

SUPERIOR

The Cardinal could do whatever he wants then—he's above all, and I am going this very moment to write to inform him about your rebelling—my sister, go back to your post.

NUN

Yes, my mother.

(looking at Helene)

Ah! What a little thing possessed by Satan.

SUPERIOR

We will discipline her.

(The Superior goes back into the building—the nun leaves by the right.)

HELENE (alone)

So there's no more hope then, and my benefactress—it's because I was devoted to her that they've separated me from her. The Marquise must have that ring in two days. Can Mr. D'Artagnan have succeeded in his action? Will he bring back those priceless jewels? But, even if he had them in his possession, he doesn't know for whom they are destined, he knows only me. And how to let him know that they've got me locked up in this convent? Poor young man!

(sings)

Soul filled with hope—no question

Proud of possessing his treasure

He thinks at the end of his road

That he's going to find me again!

In the interest of the enterprise

I wish that he might know all

First of all to save the Marquise

And then to see him again, a bit

(The entry bell rings.)

SUPERIOR (emerging from the house)

Who comes again to disturb the calm of our retreat?

(to Helene)

Lower your veil, Miss.

NUN

Madame Superior—there are five pilgrims demanding asylum.

SUPERIOR

Five pilgrims! Heaven illuminates us with Grace! Quickly, bring in these men of God, my sister—

HELENE

Do you permit me a stroll in the garden, Madame?

SUPERIOR

A twenty-minute stroll, I agree to it.

HELENE (aside)

Let's figure out some way. Ah! If Mr. D'Artagnan were here—he would have already saved us all.

(she goes into the garden)

SUPERIOR

Oh? I'll keep a sharp watch on that one. But here are our visitors.

(Enter Athos, Porthos, Aramis, Planchet, and D'Artagnan disguised as Pilgrims.)

THE YOUNG MEN (singing)

In this asylum

Sweet and peaceful

From travel

Protected shelter—

Deign, from grace

To grant room

To pilgrims

Lost on the highway.

ARAMIS

For our sacred speech.

ATHOS

For our successful faith.

PORTHOS

Everywhere—oh, saintly nation, we have been revered.

D'ARTAGNAN

And no one in your home

Will have, I bet,

In his entire life have met

Pilgrims like us—

(Refrain)

In this asylum, etc.

NUN (looking at them)

What an air of beatitude.

PLANCHET (greeting the nun and making grimaces)

I kiss your feet, my sister.

SUPERIOR

Be welcome, my brothers, are you coming from far away?

PORTHOS (low to D'Artagnan)

From where are we coming?

D'ARTAGNAN (aloud)

From Palestine, my sister.

SUPERIOR

Ah! How lucky you are! You have seen the Holy Land.

ATHOS

Just the way we see you.

PORTHOS

I've even brought a little of it in my pocket.

SUPERIOR

Will you be so kind as to give me a pinch?

PORTHOS

Very gladly, my sister.

(low to others)

I will give her some tobacco.

ARAMIS

But as it's really a long way from here—also, we are very weary.

PLANCHET

With what we've made the whole way on foot.

(Porthos pushes Planchet.)

SUPERIOR

On foot? I thought that to go to Palestine you had to cross the sea?

PLANCHET

Oh! A very small sea!

SUPERIOR

Ah! My brothers, we really need your presence to bring back to us a stray lamb.

ARAMIS

A young lamb?

ATHOS

A pretty lamb?

PORTHOS

A strong lamb?

SUPERIOR

Eighteen years old and pretty as a Madonna.

D'ARTAGNAN

We are going to confess her.

SUPERIOR

A moment, my brothers, you must need to get back your strength.

PORTHOS

Oh! Yes! I'd really like to eat something.

SUPERIOR

We're going to serve you a light meal under this grove.

ATHOS

Can't we see the sheep in question while waiting?

SUPERIOR

Later, my brothers. Nourishment for the soul after that of the body.

D'ARTAGNAN

In that case, hurry up, by Jove!

SUPERIOR

Huh?

D'ARTAGNAN (back in his part)

I was saying that we were in haste to be agreeable to you, My

Mother.

SUPERIOR (to the Nun)

The saintly men! It delays them to enter in prayer. What a treasure for the convent.

(sings)

My brothers, be patient

As for me, I am going with this step

To proceed with diligence

In the preparation of your repast.

D'ARTAGNAN

Count on our pious zeal

If you have in this convent

Still some rebellious sheep

Send her to us straight away.

(Refrain)

Have confidence in us

Heaven guided our step here

And be sure our eloquence

Will not weaken hereabouts.

(The Superior and the Nun leave.)

D'ARTAGNAN

At last we can talk. Ah! My friends, it's because of you I am no longer the prisoner of the Marquis.

PORTHOS

Hardly, had we made the Count escape—when we realized you were caught—we retraced our steps to free you—it's quite simple.

ARAMIS

The Marquis made you leave for Paris under escort by six men. We awaited their passage in a side road.

PORTHOS

We exploded like lightening on your guards—we roughed 'em up.

D'ARTAGNAN

Ah! Here I am free—ah! My, friends—what don't I owe you?

PORTHOS

What are you talking about?

(sings)

Can it be your heart forgets

The oaths we've taken?

The same fate links us.

Pain, pleasure, loud swearing

Come what may in life—

Henceforth all is common between us.

THE OTHERS

Henceforth all is common between us.

PORTHOS

Do friends of our age hesitate?

No—we had to break your slavery

To reanimate our courage

We thought on the oath we took

No peril can be remembered

When one fights for friendship's sake.

ALL

No peril can be remembered

When one fights for friendship's sake.

ARAMIS

All the same gentlemen, we did quite well after that to assume this pilgrim's costume, that a saintly man wanted to give us—

that will put those who are sent in pursuit after us—off the track.

D'ARTAGNAN

And that gave us entry into this monastery where we can rest until this evening—but not for long after that, because we must be in Paris to deliver this ring—let's not forget it!

PORTHOS

We have time to have a good meal—one must really dine here, they say the nuns are very fond of good food.

PLANCHET

There's only one thing that bothers me—it's that we lost that unfortunate Pelotte on the way. She stopped to sew some pants. There's still mending for her to do.

D'ARTAGNAN

We'll find her again—in any event, she'll join us in Paris—but pay heed—someone's coming—will it be that young lamb?

PORTHOS

No—it's an old nanny-goat.

NUN

With basket and setting a table in the grove. My Brothers, here's your light meal.

PORTHOS

She came very much apropos. See—see—

(he goes to see what's been placed on the table)

Ah! My God: hazelnuts—

ATHOS

Dry raisins.

ARAMIS

Figs.

D'ARTAGNAN

Small cakes—it appears that the good sisters take us for canaries.

PLANCHET

Some Spanish liquorices.

PORTHOS

And plain water.

PLANCHET

We will make some coco!

NUN

Regale yourselves, my Brothers.

(She leaves.)

ATHOS

Now there's a feast.

PLANCHET

We won't get drunk.

D'ARTAGNAN (sings)

Fresh figs, hazelnuts.

ATHOS (sings)

Some almonds, dried raisins.

PORTHOS

I'd have preferred cutlets or fowl or beef. God! How I'd like some beef.

ARAMIS

Can one be eloquent after eating such stuff!

D'ARTAGNAN

All that you can do after this is to preach on abstinence.

PORTHOS

Why this is frightful—to dine with this—not even preserves—no liquors—and they say that nuns make very good sweetmeats.

ATHOS

It's not possible that they only live on hazelnuts—they must have hiding places where they put their appetizers.

ARAMIS

Gentlemen, suppose we try to discover it. Suppose we slip into the refectory.

PLANCHET

Oh—that's the thing—we'll also try to find the cellar, and if these lay sisters meet us, we'll convert 'em.

D'ARTAGNAN

Go. As for me, I'm remaining here—I'll keep watch.

ALL

Tally ho!

(singing)

Let's hesitate no more

We must, without losing one single moment

Put the provisions of this convent

To pillage and plunder.

(They all go inside except D'Artagnan.)

D'ARTAGNAN

So long as they don't let themselves be surprised! Ah—as for me, I'm in a hurry to be in Paris, to see my charming protectress again and to ask if she is satisfied with me.

HELENE (emerging from the gardens)

The time they granted me has expired—I must go back in—ah! A pilgrim.

D'ARTAGNAN

Someone—Great God!

HELENE

Mr. D'Artagnan!

D'ARTAGNAN

Madame Helene!

(sings)

What! It's you I see again. Ah! What happiness! What intoxication! It's your hand I press.

TOGETHER

I fear nothing this time.

D'ARTAGNAN

Ah! I will go crazy, I think.

HELENE

But what chance, what mystery?

D'ARTAGNAN

You, in this solitary place? What joy!

HELENE

Thanks my God. You heard my prayer.

(refrain)

What, it's you I see again?

D'ARTAGNAN

You—in this convent—thirty leagues from Paris—

HELENE

But you—this pilgrim's costume?

D'ARTAGNAN

We had to assume it with my friends to escape those who were pursuing us. I will explain about this to you—much later.

HELENE

Above all, put an end to my impatience—have you succeeded in your enterprise—and that ring?

D'ARTAGNAN

Here it is, Miss—Mr. de Grammont entrusted it to me.

HELENE

This is it! This is actually it! Ah, I really knew, that nothing was impossible to him, and that he would save the Marquise.

D'ARTAGNAN (presenting the ring to her.)

Take this jewel, Miss—which is so impatiently awaited.

HELENE

No—no—on the contrary, keep it. I will tell you to whom you must take it. For I am a prisoner here.

D'ARTAGNAN (after having replaced the ring in his pocket)

Prisoner! And who dares to keep you here?

HELENE

Cardinal Richelieu—he's separated me from the Marquise and had me taken to this cloister whose gates are impossible to force.

D'ARTAGNAN

Impossible! Oh! I'll answer for you indeed—that I will tear you from this place.

HELENE

Think of what you are saying! Struggle with the Cardinal?

D'ARTAGNAN

To free you, I will battle with the devil.

HELENE

As brave as generous!

D'ARTAGNAN

Oh! I take my oath right here to carry you off from this convent, and you know whether I keep my word!

(sings)

When you said to me "Leave,

To avert a great misfortune

And to reach success

You need brains and courage."

I fled your cherished presence

And on my breast, where I returned shone the tutelary ring.

Have I kept my word?

HELENE

Yes, chevalier full of valor

You risked everything for us.

D'ARTAGNAN

Didn't I—as a reward—have on my return, a very sweet prize? That prize, that supreme favor, are you thinking of it now?

HELENE (lowering her eyes)

It's a kiss.

D'ARTAGNAN

That's the one.

HELENE (offers her cheek that D'Artagnan kisses.)

Have I kept my oath?

D'ARTAGNAN

Ah! By Jove, that kiss will make me throw down these walls.

HELENE

No imprudence, Mr. D'Artagnan. Trust me—leave quickly for Paris; hurry to deliver this ring to the Marquise. She must have it within three days.

D'ARTAGNAN

No, no—oh! We will leave together.

HELENE

Yet once more, how can you hope?

D'ARTAGNAN

I don't know at all, but with an iron will and devoted friends.

HELENE

What? Your friends are here?

D'ARTAGNAN

They are getting supplies—wait, I hear them.

(Porthos, Athos, Aramis, and Planchet return—one has a pot of jam, the other a pot of butter, another a jar of pickles, the other ring bagels.)

TOGETHER

Ah—a truly great hunt —exquisite delicacies. Fill our pockets, it's ravishing, yes, it's the dessert of the convent.

ATHOS

I've got butter.

ARAMIS

We will relish this jam.

PORTHOS

These jams—these bagels, these macaroons.

PLANCHET

As for me, I've found gherkins.

(refrain)

Ah, a truly great hunt, etc.

PORTHOS (spoken)

With all this we shall make a famous meal—I'd have preferred a shank of lamb.

D'ARTAGNAN

Eh! Gentlemen, it's really a question of thinking of a repast when we have a lady to save.

ALL (noticing Helene)

A lady!

ATHOS

Oh! How pretty she is.

ARAMIS

Would this be the lamb in question?

D'ARTAGNAN

My friends, salute the charming incognito for whom we undertook this voyage.

HELENE

Who is quite delighted to find you here to express to you her gratitude.

D'ARTAGNAN

You shall thank us after we have rendered you free.

ATHOS

What? Is it that Miss—?

D'ARTAGNAN

Is detained here by order of the Cardinal—but we will free her, right?

PORTHOS

We swear it.

HELENE

By what means—?

PORTHOS

We have no idea, but that doesn't matter.

ALL

We swear it.

D'ARTAGNAN

Ah—wait—if we could yet—that's it—we all have pilgrim's robes—by taking one of our costumes—we will wait until night, we will leave the convent, you will leave with us.

PLANCHET

Ah! Yes, but the one who will have given his costume—he'll have to remain.

ATHOS

Big deal—that will be you.

PLANCHET

What d'ya mean, me?

ALL

Yes, yes, it's agreed.

PLANCHET

Ah! Excuse me, gentlemen, as soon as I am discovered and the nuns administer correction to me—thanks.

D'ARTAGNAN

No reflection—you will give your robe or we will suppress your wages.

HELENE

But, even if I could disguise myself, at night they lock me in my cell—whose window is there—

(pointing)

How to get out of it?

D'ARTAGNAN

The window has no bars—it's only on the second floor—you will make it short—we will mount on Planchet.

PLANCHET

Great, me again! Here I am becoming a footstool now.

D'ARTAGNAN

This evening at nine o'clock.

PORTHOS

Here's the Superior—attention.

(They move away from Helene.)

SUPERIOR

Ah! Miss is with you, my brothers. So much the better. Have you instructed her with the feeling of respect that she owes us?

D'ARTAGNAN

Yes, my sister, and we have found this young novice very docile to our instruction.

PORTHOS

And she asks nothing better than to follow our instructions.

SUPERIOR

God be praised. You beatify me. But take your meal, my

brothers.

(violent ringing)

Again, someone outside, who can be coming to us so late?

PORTHOS

Come on, let's eat our hazelnuts for lack of better, and let's try to prevent her from seeing the jam.

(All five sit at the table.)

NUN (running)

Madame Superior, it's a great lord, sent by His Eminence. He insists on speaking to you right away. It's about Madame Helene.

HELENE

About me!

SUPERIOR

And the name of this Lord?

NUN

Here he is himself.

HELENE (aside)

The Marquis.

D'ARTAGNAN (low to the others)

Monsieur de Franconnard—let's hide carefully under our robes and push our hats over our eyes.

MARQUIS (bowing)

Madame Superior, receive the salutations of the Marquis de Franconnard. Ah! Here exactly, this dear Helene—it's for you, little one, that I have come here.

HELENE

For me, sir?

MARQUIS

No question. Pressed again yesterday by me to adorn herself with the ring that she obtained from the munificence of the Cardinal, the Marquise confessed to me, Miss, that she had confided this ring to you.

HELENE

It's true, there was a loose stone. The ring is in Paris.

MARQUIS

It's so you can deliver it to the Marquise that the Prime Minister has agreed to set you at liberty. Here's the order which has dispatched me.

(he gives it to the Superior)

HELENE

I am free!

SUPERIOR

It's signed by the Cardinal, Sir—you can take Miss away.

MARQUIS

Well, my child—go make your preparations. Take your time, I won't be annoyed to rest a bit and take something. I am harassed and I'm dying of need.

SUPERIOR

If Milord would like to share the repast of these pious pilgrims.

MARQUIS

Ah, pilgrims—I didn't have the honor of seeing them.

(he bows to them)

My brothers, certainly, I will be flattered.

(he looks at the table)

But it seems a bit thin to me, your feast. For pilgrims, I conceive that it's called a repast, but for me I really don't like dried fruits and plain water.

SUPERIOR

It's the best we have to offer you here.

MARQUIS

Oh! I am well provided for at dinner—since a certain adventure that happened to me in Cahors, a pullet that they whisked away from me, I no longer embark without biscuits.

(to Valets)

Lapierre, Jean, return to my carriage and bring a pâté here—a fowl and some flasks of wine. You will allow me, mother?

SUPERIOR

Yes, sir—on the condition that all these prohibited things do not enter the interior of this house.

MARQUIS

That won't be a problem—I will eat here with these pilgrims—they will make a small place for me at their table.

PORTHOS

Willingly.

(aside)

We will do better than that.

SUPERIOR (to Helene)

Come make your preparation my girl, so as to be ready to leave.

(The Superior goes in with Helene, who is watching the young men. The valet brings provisions and bottles.)

MARQUIS

Ah! Very good. Place all that on this table. You will excuse me, respectable pilgrims—this does not offend you?

D'ARTAGNAN

Oh—not at all—to the contrary.

PORTHOS

What a scout, what a nice look.

ATHOS

Will you sit down, my brother?

ARAMIS

We are very honored with your company.

MARQUIS

These pilgrims are very well brought up.

(sits at the table)

Imagine, my brother, that I need to refresh myself, because I've been running since this morning after five bad scamps, who played me a hang-worthy trick.

D'ARTAGNAN (taking some pâté, as do the others)

Oh! Truly—and you've caught them?

MARQUIS

Why no, it's they who caught me! Hey, you are eating pâté, my brothers.

PORTHOS (mouth full)

Yes, we are tasting it.

ARAMIS

So as to mortify ourselves.

D'ARTAGNAN

We've taken a vow to eat whatever is served at our table.

PLANCHET

It might be stones that we would eat.

MARQUIS

Ah! Bah! Really?

PORTHOS

But I prefer this to stones.

MARQUIS (aside)

Ah, indeed! Why, these good pilgrims are devouring all of my pate—there isn't any more for me.

D'ARTAGNAN

Have some of these figs, my brother.

MARQUIS

Thanks, thanks, but I prefer the fowl if you would pass it to me.

PORTHOS

Ah! Allow me—I want to have the honor of slicing it.

(he slices)

MARQUIS

Are you coming from far away, my brothers?

D'ARTAGNAN

From Mecca, and we took a vow to continually go two steps forward and four backward.

MARQUIS

Ah, you went two steps forward and four—son of a gun—why in that case I ask myself how you got here—it seems to me very difficult.

D'ARTAGNAN

Not at all—we were walking backwards.

(Porthos has served everyone, he gives the Marquis a slice of skin.)

MARQUIS

Ah, very well, I understand now. I'm with you—it's all the same—it must give you a stiff neck to be always looking behind oneself.

(he looks at his plate)

Skin! All there remains for me is skin—ah! Indeed! Why they are ogres, these pilgrim.

PORTHOS

Something to drink?

ALL

Something to drink!

(They pour themselves wine.)

MARQUIS

And they are drinking my wine—these are strange anchorites.

THE YOUNG MEN (singing)

Ah—this wine is divine.

Let's drink (repeat)

And clink—!

Empty the bottles,

We must do honor (repeat)

To Milord.

MARQUIS (holding out his glass)

Give me, from kindness, some of this delectable wine.

PORTHOS

Ah—that's very just, really, you've deserved it—

MARQUIS (aside)

Ah—this will soon end. I swear it by the devil! If I'm ever caught again dining with a pilgrim.

(refrain)

Ah, wine, etc.

SUPERIOR (entering)

Milord—here's Miss Helene, who's ready to follow you.

MARQUIS (rising from the table)

Gladly, because to have a meal like this one, I prefer to be on my way.

D'ARTAGNAN (rising with his companions)

My sister, we are also going to take leave of you—and my brothers, by thanking you for your hospitality.

SUPERIOR

Take leave of us! Why you cannot leave for a week. The rule

of this monastery is strict, you are going to be in retreat and in prayers.

THE YOUNG MEN

Ah! My God!

HELENE (aside)

And I haven't taken the ring.

PORTHOS

To pray for eight days!

PLANCHET

We'll have time to eat hazelnuts.

D'ARTAGNAN

Why, my sister—we were unaware of this custom and we cannot—

SUPERIOR

You ought to have known it. In any event you must abide by it—

MARQUIS

Yes, yes, Oh! That's the rule, I know it myself. Besides, it seems to me now that you can indeed fast quite a time—you've had an advance. Let's leave, Miss.

HELENE (aside, giving her arm to the Marquis)

Ah, the Marquise is lost.

D'ARTAGNAN (to others)

She's going away and I still have the ring.

PLANCHET (low)

It's all over with us.

D'ARTAGNAN

Not yet. We will get out of here—if we have to set fire to the convent.

SUPERIOR

Pray for us, my brothers.

(All the nuns fall to their knees before the pilgrims while the Marquis leads Helen [who's making signs to D'Artagnan] away.)

CHORUS

Good Pilgrims, may the Lord inflame

So as to make the malign spirit within us depart

And in this moment, implore for our souls.

You see we are all at your knees.

CURTAIN

ACT V

A rich room at the Marquis' palace—door at the back and side door.

ANGELIQUE (to Helene, who enters by the rear)

Well, Helene—?

HELENE

Nothing yet, Madame.

ANGELIQUE

What, no news—?

HELENE

None—I've come from Mr. D'Artagnan's and they told me neither he nor his friends have reappeared.

ANGELIQUE

They must have been forced to remain for a week in that convent where you told me you had left them.

HELENE

Poor young kids! What a penitence.

ANGELIQUE

And in two hours, the Marquis is going to come find me to take me to the Cardinal—if I don't have that ring—judge the wrath of His Eminence and that of my husband—who cannot fail to discover everything—I will be ruined!

HELENE

Be courageous, Madame, we've still got two hours and that's more than these brave young men need to accomplish this mission.

(sings)

Don't give up all hope

In them, I am still confident!

I'll answer to you for their fortitude

They have heart

And honor

During a whole week

They, languishing in a monastery!

No—no—from this austere exile

They will have gaily extracted themselves

With cleverness

Deceiving the Abbess.

Their gentility

Will aid them

In its clemency,

Providence,

To save you, will bring them.

ANGELIQUE

Generous children—to expose themselves thus for me, who they don't know.

HELENE (lowering her eyes)

Ah—there's one of 'em who knows me.

ANGELIQUE

I understand—it's to you they are rendering service—never mind—I could never prove my gratitude to them sufficiently.

HELENE

You've already begun by making them obtain what they desire with so much ardor—what will be their joy, their surprise when they find on their return these commissions and these brilliant uniforms that you have purchased for them.

ANGELIQUE (walking about in agitation without hearing her)

Another ten minutes gone! And no one.

HELENE

They're coming—

A SERVANT (entering)

The Marquis is coming to ask if Madame would be willing to see him.

ANGELIQUE

Eh, what! Already—

(to valet)

Tell the Marquis that I am finishing dressing.

HELENE

Try to gain some time—as for me, I will run one last time to the lodging of our saviors—who knows? Perhaps they will have returned.

ANGELIQUE

Go, my good Helene—I have no more hope except you.

HELENE

Drive from your heart this terror that freezes it, the peril which threatens. It will emerge the conqueror!

Nothing to fear.

Let hope replace it.

Often a little audacity leads us to happiness.

ANGELIQUE

I feel I've born in my heart a terror that freezes it

Of the peril that threatens

I see the depth

Nothing of fear!

Let hope replace it!

Often a bit of audacity

Leads us to joy.

(Helene leaves by a side door. The Marquis enters from the back.)

MARQUIS

What, Marquise, you haven't yet finished dressing?

ANGELIQUE

No, Sir—some flowers are to be added to my headdress.

MARQUIS

Truly, you young girls are so slow—you don't know that the

Cardinal's going to take us in his carriage of four or six horses—a magnificent coupling—

ANGELIQUE

Ah—

MARQUIS

Yes, Madame, in his own carriage with his own stallions. That astonishes you? Me, too—I am speechless, choked by the good graces of His Eminence; since our marriage Cardinal de Richelieu is so kind regarding me—he began by making me his grand squire—and he promised to make me something more later.

ANGELIQUE (aside)

Helene is not returning.

MARQUIS

In the end, you yourself have seen that he refuses me nothing—witness these four commissions of Musketeers that you begged me to solicit for I don't know who—

ANGELIQUE

And this petition that I ordered you to deliver to the Queen—

MARQUIS

It was given to her at her sports—I'm unaware too, what it contained—but these are your secrets, Angelique, and I respect your diplomacy— All that I ask is that you present to the Cardinal your hand adorned with the ring he made you a present of—for he said to me this morning, fixing the hour of this reception, "Marquise de Franconnard, that I would see with pleasure that she adorns herself with that jewel I had the honor of offering her." And he showed me this wish with a manner which was equivalent to an order.

ANGELIQUE (aside)

He is implacable.

MARQUIS (looking at the Marquise's hand)

Why what's this—you still don't have that ring?

ANGELIQUE (embarrassed)

No—Sir—it's at the jewelers. Helene won't delay bringing it to me.

MARQUIS

So long as she doesn't fail—without it, we would be disgraced—go quickly to finish your dressing, Angelique—only an hour remains to you—

ANGELIQUE (aside)

One hour! It's over—they will get here too late.

MARQUIS (sings)

The Cardinal awaits us

Finish getting dressed

Do everything, at the moment

So as to be a coquette!

ANGELIQUE

The Cardinal awaits us. How uneasy my mind is. It will soon conjure up a storm over us.

(The Marquise goes into the room at the right.)

MARQUIS (alone)

I am going to be in the pink of favor—meaning that I am on the point of becoming extremely powerful—if I didn't fear for my outfit, I would allow myself a slight pirouette. Ah! Bah! I will permit it—besides, that's done at court—one pirouettes a lot.

(He pirouettes and stops in the middle.)

SERVANT (entering)

Milord, there's a flower girl who insists on speaking to you—

MARQUIS

A flower girl. I have nothing to disentangle with a type like that—tell me, is the slut pretty?

SERVANT

Charming, Milord.

MARQUIS

Then show her in.

(Servant leaves.)

MARQUIS

Since she's nice, I am going to make Angelique a present of a bouquet—that will please the Cardinal.

PELOTTE (in the wings)

You say that he is the Marquis? That's fine—Thanks.

MARQUIS

Heavens—that laryngeal organ is no stranger to me.

PELOTTE (curtsying)

Milord, I have indeed the honor—

MARQUIS (recognizing her)

Ah! My little calf from the environs of La Rochelle!

PELOTTE

The same, Milord.

MARQUIS

What! It's you, little one! Still as fresh! Also as plump.

(he takes her by the waist)

PELOTTE

And you, still as lecherous.

MARQUIS

What do you want? It's from the saltpeter that flows in my vertebrae—I have a vitriolic temperament.

PELOTTE

You must take cold baths—that will calm you down.

MARQUIS

Eh! Eh! Still malicious. Ah! Ah! Why I thought you were a clothes-mender—

PELOTTE

No question— Well?

MARQUIS

Well—these bouquets—

PELOTTE

Ah! It's time—I've changed jobs—the profession of clothes-mender wasn't doing well—breeches are of a ridiculous fidelity these days—you no longer find holey pants.

.MARQUIS

No more holey pants! What a glory for the hoosiers.

PELOTTE

So—I'm now a flower girl.

(sings)

Yes, now, I'm a flower girl. It's a profession that does well in all. You should see me when my voice is weak.

From all sides comes barges. Everywhere on my passage. Each rends me homage. Beautiful flowers, nice face. I have something for all tastes. I am giving to our coquettes lilies, daisies. Roses in garlands. Worries for husbands.

MARQUIS

She sets me on fire! But now I think of it, what brings me the pleasure of seeing you again?

PELOTTE

Hell, you told me that I had only to say a word, that you would make my fortune—that you make a pet of me.

MARQUIS

Not here, not here—in my little house—right—I will put you in what you wish— But in my residence, in the face of my wife—! I can only put you out the door and that's all—

PELOTTE

You didn't grasp me.

MARQUIS

Besides—your four little good-for-nothing protectors would have only to guess my intentions—

PELOTTE

I repeat to you that you are going astray. When you spoke to me of fortune, I believed you weren't scheming any malice—in proof of which I came to ask you for a job for my intended.

MARQUIS

Your intended? You have an intended?

PELOTTE

Yes, and I desire that he be entered into Milord's livery.

MARQUIS

Ah! You want him to wear my livery—don't worry, I will make him wear them.

(aside)

That's a pretext so she can get close to me. She is sharp like a fox.

PELOTTE

May I introduce my intended, Milord? He is there—but you know him—you already met him in a fisherman's cabana near La Rochelle.

MARQUIS

Ah! Yes—he was in the service of your four bad actors.

PELOTTE

That's exactly the same one.

MARQUIS

Introduce him—in petto.

PELOTTE (calling)

Planchet! Planchet!

MARQUIS (aside, laughing)

In this manner morality is satisfied. I will put him in the kitchen—my spouse will see only fire there—

PLANCHET (to servant, who bars his entry)

Since—I tell you Pelotte called me—hold on, even she is there—

MARQUIS (to Servant)

Japreso—let him in.

(The Servant disappears.)

PLANCHET (bowing)

Milord, I repose my respects.

MARQUIS (laughing)

Ah! Ah! Ah! Excellent kind of husband! Yes, I recognize him—still the same air of felicity.

PLANCHET

Milord has not changed either.

MARQUIS

And what's become of those four little comedians, of whom you were, I believe, the groom, good-for-nothing?

PLANCHET (weeping)

Hi, hi, hi, hi!

MARQUIS

He's whining!

PELOTTE (weeping, too)

Hi, hi, hi, hi—!

MARQUIS

And Pelotte, too! Look, what happened to them that's so troubling?

PELOTTE

Don't speak to me of it—

PLANCHET AND PELOTTE

Hi, hi, hi, hi! If you knew.

MARQUIS

What? What?

PLANCHET

Imagine that in returning from La Rochelle we found in front of a large ditch—which served as an enclosure—there was a bridge to get over it, but it was too far—these gentlemen who were on horseback—shouted, "Leap the ditch." In vain I told them, "Believe me, take the bridge." They didn't hear me—they urged on their horses—but when they were in the air they realized they weren't going to reach the other side—then they tried to turn back, but the horses, not being prepared for this maneuver, fell into the ditch—where I left them.

MARQUIS (delighted)

Truly? Ah, so much the better! I rejoice over that. They got what they deserved! But while waiting here, you are without employment, and you would like to enter my service?

PLANCHET

I admit—that I would flatter myself enough over it.

MARQUIS

Then thank your fiancée, for I am granting you that honor.

PLANCHET

Ah! Ah! Milord!

PELOTTE

How kind!

MARQUIS

You will live here in my home—

PLANCHET

Ah! Ah! Milord.

MARQUIS

With your wife!

PLANCHET

Ah! Ah! Milord

MARQUIS

If you are sweet to me, I will be the relative of all your children—and I plan for you to have 'em every year.

PLANCHET

Ah! That's enough—truly—Milord takes my measure very well.

PELOTTE

He overwhelms us—but with all that, Milord has not yet so much as bought one bouquet from me.

MARQUIS

My word, you're right—and as for me, I intended to offer one to the Marquise.

(he takes a bouquet which she holds)

Now there's something that pleases me.

PELOTTE (taking the bouquet back and presenting him with another)

Oh! No, Milord, not that—hold on—here's the one that must be for Madame—

MARQUIS

Why this one? I preferred the other one.

PELOTTE

It's that this one is more gallant.

(much lower)

And I made it at your instruction.

MARQUIS

That's different. You'll tell me more about it.

PELOTTE

Alas, heck! It is elaborately done.

(sings)

You'll meet roses there,

Violets, carnations, marguerites, half-open daisies, lilies.

MARQUIS (sings)

Yes, from this pretty gift from Flora. Flowers have for me a thousand allures.

(looking at Pelotte meaningfully)

But I find still more beautiful

That which isn't found there.

PLANCHET

Ah! Ah! Milord.

MARQUIS

Yes, yes, that's sufficiently witty.

PELOTTE

I notice a great lady heading this way.

MARQUIS

That's my noble spouse.

ANGELIQUE

I don't see Helene and the hour has struck.

MARQUIS (giving the bouquet)

Ah! Angelique—allow me to offer you this bouquet—that I ordered for you from this little one—she has been on time. I will give her my business.

PELOTTE

If Madame is content—that's all that I desire.

(aside)

She's hardly looking at it!

MARQUIS

But what—nothing on your finger? Helen has not returned yet?

ANGELIQUE

Not yet.

MARQUIS

I am on burning coals.

CARDINAL'S SQUIRE

The Carriage of His Eminence is at the gate of the Hotel.

MARQUIS

And the Cardinal is going to be impatient. See if the little one has come back.

ANGELIQUE (aside)

What to do?

PLANCHET (low)

If I dared to make signs to her—

PELOTTE

She's not looking at us.

ANGELIQUE (going quickly to Helene, who enters)

Ah! Helene.

(Helene does not reply and lowers her eyes)

I understand—all is lost.

MARQUIS (noticing Helene)

Helene! All is saved—

Give—quickly give that jewel, Miss.

PELOTTE (going to Helene and speaking low to her)

Tell Madame la Marquise to look in her bouquet.

HELENE (low to Angelique)

In the bouquet!

ANGELIQUE (searing in the bouquet and finding the ring)

Ah!

MARQUIS

Well—

ANGELIQUE

Well! Milord, here's this ring—you see plainly I am putting it on my finger.

MARQUIS

Ah! Bravo! Bravo! You frightened me.

ANGELIQUE (low to Helene)

Saved! Saved!

A SERVANT (entering)

Milord, four musketeers are asking to present their respects to you.

MARQUIS

Four musketeers!

A SERVANT

Messrs D'Artagnan, Athos, Porthos, and Aramis.

MARQUIS

I don't know these musketeers and I haven't the time—

ANGELIQUE

They are the young men for whom you obtained these commissions; they are coming to thank you. You cannot avoid seeing them.

MARQUIS

Ah! They are your protégés—let them be shown in—I won't be sorry to know these gentlemen that I've enlisted as musketeers.

(Enter the four young men in uniform as musketeers.)

THE YOUNG MEN (sing)

Ah! For your tutelary kindness,

We come to thank you all

For if we are musketeers

Milord, it's actually thanks to you.

MARQUIS (bowing)

Gentlemen—certainly I am quite charmed. Ah! Indeed—why I'm not dreaming. These are my four demons—and I'm the one who enlisted them as musketeers.

D'ARTAGNAN

Believe, Milord Marquis—that we are preserving eternal gratitude for that.

PORTHOS (speaking as a pilgrim)

Yes, Milord—and if we return to Mecca, it will be at your order.

MARQUIS

To Mecca—they were also those gourmands of pilgrims—ah, indeed—for you weren't killed in the ditch?

THE YOUNG MEN

In the ditch?

ATHOS

What ditch?

ARAMIS

We don't understand, Milord.

MARQUIS (to Planchet)

What was it that you told me, you imbecile?

PLANCHET

Milord, I must have had a vision—

ANGELIQUE (to Count de Grammont who enters)

Ah—Count de Grammont.

COUNT (to Angelique)

Yes, Madame—the Queen at your prayer, has obtained my pardon—and I am coming to thank you.

MARQUIS (noticing the Count)

Eh! Now here's that dear Grammont—so you are actually free—this excellent friend! That makes me pleased.

COUNT

I have no doubt of it, Marquis, since it's to you I owe my liberty.

MARQUIS

To me?

ANGELIQUE

That petition that you delivered to the queen was to ask mercy for the Count.

MARQUIS

Ah, bah!

(aside)

They made me do a whole host of things I didn't suspect.

(aloud)

Gentlemen, excuse us, but the Cardinal awaits us.

(low to Pelotte)

You'll be flower girl to the King—

PELOTTE

No, I wanted to sell only one bouquet. I'm returning to clothes mending.

MARQUIS

Then I'll promise for you all the legs of the Court.

(aloud)

Come, Angelique.

(Music. He goes upstage, the Marquise follows him, passing before the young men—she gives them her hand without saying a word.)

THE YOUNG MEN

Ah! Madame!

ATHOS, PORTHOS, ARAMIS

Glory is ours!

D'ARTAGNAN (kissing Helene's hand)

Happiness is mine.

CHORUS

Let's move away! Very promptly

Let's move away.

We must immediately

Appear before His Eminence.

(repeat)

CURTAIN

ABOUT THE TRANSLATOR

Frank J. Morlock has written and translated many plays since retiring from the legal profession in 1992. His translations have also appeared on Project Gutenberg, the Alexandre Dumas Père web page, Literature in the Age of Napoléon, Infinite Artistries.com, and Munsey's (formerly Blackmask). In 2006 he received an award from the North American Jules Verne Society for his translations of Verne's plays. He lives and works in México.

www.ingramcontent.com/pod-product-compliance
Lightning Source LLC
LaVergne TN
LVHW041618070426
835507LV00008B/313